KEEP THE FAITH

LETTERS FROM A CATHOLIC FATHER

WILLIAM R. MCNAMER

Lightning Source, Inc.
1246 Heil Quaker Blvd.
La Vergne, TN 37086

Manufactured in the United States of America

ISBN 978-0-9817297-0-1

For Bruce, Sarah and Richard,
Bridget and John, Amy and Jimmy,
Deirdre and Eric, Timothy
—and Elizabeth, with thanks and love.

Acknowledgements

Thanks to my wife Elizabeth, professor of religion, for her always helpful advice; to Fr. Armand Nigro, S.J., my inestimable mentor and theological and spiritual guide from start to finish; to Fr. Thomas Bokenkotter, Fr. Chris Hayden, and Bert Ghezzi for their review and comment; and to Sister Monica McCormilla for her help on prayer.

Also thanks to my children and their spouses for generously going through with me two rounds of critical review from the vantage point of today's young adult.

Preface

While this book as a series of letters is primarily addressed to young adult Catholics who may be having trouble hanging onto their faith, it turns out to be a concise but fairly comprehensive summary of the Catholic faith in modern terms, backed by comprehensive research and consultation (see Acknowledgements and Notes).

Therefore I think the book may also be of value to older Catholic adults, many of whom have not had the advantage of advanced education in the teaching of the Church. Much has changed since Vatican II, and there is also much underlying explanation of the Church's teaching which should be grasped.

CONTENTS

Introduction

Dear Family and Friends,

I'm a lawyer and the father of five young adult children with good education and wonderful values, some of whom are a bit wobbly about their Catholic faith right now. I write this short book on the Catholic faith in the form of letters to them—but you, my other readers, are all included as recipients of these letters.

I think with all the pressures of family and work these days it is difficult for young people to keep up the practice of the faith, especially if there is a certain level of disinterest or disbelief. Yet I know that most of you would like the faith to be a meaningful part of your lives, as it was when you were growing up Catholic.

What are the problems?

- A college education has taught you "critical thinking," yet your knowledge of the Catholic faith is at the eighth grade level. How can you possibly fit the faith into your more intellectual way of life?

- You live in a world that is hostile to faith. Some of you live in an environment that is aggressively secular. Stephen Carter, the Yale law professor, writes, "Despite all the God-talk in America, the dominant culture is essentially a quasi-pagan society that trivializes religion when it is not mocking it."

- You have many friends who are skeptics, agnostics, or even atheists, don't go to church, but are really good people. Why, then, should you go to church?

- If you have children, you practice "family values." Isn't that good enough without disrupting the weekend with Mass?

- You are mad at the Church for taking stances on sex, and on women, that you feel are unreal and chauvinistic, especially contraception, abortion, and women priests.

- You find the Mass meaningless and boring, especially the music, the homilies, and the lack of a real social dimension.

- You are interested in spirituality as opposed to religion, but don't really know what it is meant by spirituality.

To handle these problems, you need to be thinking Catholics and mature parents. You need to know what the Church really stands for, and how to deal with your children's faith in a practical and sensible way. Only then can you make responsible judgments about the role the Catholic faith will play in your own life, and that of your children.

The purpose of this book is to address these problems, and then go on to present a coherent explanation of the faith at an adult level, including a discussion of spirituality and Catholic lifestyle.

I am not unmindful of the marvelous generosity shown by your generation in helping those in need, and your great interest in spirituality. As out Lord would say, "You are not far from the Kingdom of Heaven." I hope to show that the Catholic faith is really about serving those in need, and about the spiritual life and the practice of the presence of God, no matter what other problems you may have with the Church.

Who am I to be writing this book? My analytical background as a lawyer helps, but mainly I'm just a practicing Catholic and a father, which I think puts me in close touch with the subject, and with you. However, my mentor throughout this project has been a Jesuit theologian and retreat master, and my wife, a professor of religious studies, has kept me in line. And I've done a great deal of specific research for this book, as you can see from the notes.

I should insert here, for the few who don't know, that the references to Vatican II are to the General Council of the Church held in Rome in the years 1962-1965, which made profound changes in the teachings and practices of the Church.

I would also add, by way of disclaimer, that I don't pretend to be some kind of a "holy Joe" who practices to perfection all that is said in this book about Catholic life. Like the rest of us, I just do my best and hope it's good enough.

Good luck and God bless,

WRM

Prologue

THE NEED FOR RELIGION AND MYSTERY IN LIFE

Why be religious at all? I think the answer is self evident. Unless we are totally ego-blind, we know we are surrounded by a Reality that is a lot bigger than we are. We know there has to be more to life than just getting through it. We long for meaning and purpose in this life and beyond. In our heart, we don't really think it's over when it's over, or what's the point?

Despite the sufferings and tragedies of life, when we look around and see love in each other and all the beauty in life, it's hard not to believe there is a loving Creator-God who made us and made all this love and beauty, that we are dependent on this God, and that we want to know more about this God. If this God is our creator, then what does God have in mind? What is God's meaning and purpose? What is our meaning and purpose? That is the quest of religion, and that is the subject of this book.

Mystery is the other part of this. If you are too earthbound to allow mystery into your life, then perhaps you are wasting your time with religion. Religion calls for a bit of poetry, a certain openness to experience of the beyond, a fondness for familiar ritual and symbol which encapsulate another dimension of reality, the dimension of mystery and even awe.

This other dimension is the spiritual dimension, the world of an infinite God who knows no limits. Such a God can be and act in ways that are beyond our finite human comprehension. Catholicism does not say we cannot understand mystery at all. Rather, that we can understand the truth of mystery, but not the fullness of that truth.

So my suggestion in approaching the concepts and practices of religion, and of Catholicism in particular, is to put on hold any *a priori* beliefs you may hold about the limits of reality. Be open to thinking outside the box. Be ready for the mystical reality of life.

Love is His Meaning

-Julian of Norwich

We shall not cease from exploration
And the end of all our exploring
Will be to arrive where we started
And know the place for the first time

-T.S. Eliot

Letter 1: Identity

Dear Family:

This series of letters is intended to be an apologetic. That's from the Greek word, *defense*, meaning a reasoned argument for Catholic belief and practice.

Nevertheless, I will make an effort not to be *argumentative*. I respect your good will and your integrity. Once in a while, however, I may have to be a bit didactic in order to keep this reasonably short.

We start with Catholic identity. Most people who have a Catholic background, whether or not they are practicing the faith, like the symbols and rituals and imagery of the Church. They feel a sense of pride when the liturgy is beautifully performed, especially when Protestant guests are present, such as at weddings and funerals. They like the Church's appeal to the senses: the color of the stained glass and vestments, the smell of incense, the sound of Gregorian chant (*keep dreaming, Dad*). They like the "poetry" of Catholicism.

And most Catholics appreciate the tradition and sense of history that pervades everything Catholic. So let's talk a bit about your own place in Catholic history and tradition.

You go back a long ways. You were born into the Roman Catholic heritage, the oldest Christian tradition in the West. The Church traces its history in unbroken descent from the Apostles of Jesus. It left the blood of its martyrs in the Roman sand. It inspired hundreds of saints down through the ages to give their entire lives to God. You inherited this tradition from generations of Catholics who have gone before you, living and dying in the faith.

You absorbed this tradition as you grew up. You learned to bless yourselves with the sign of the cross, how to say the Our Father and the Hail Mary, and the regular habit of saying grace before meals. You each had a crucifix in your bedroom. We all went to Mass as a family every Sunday.

You went to Confession and came clean about fighting with each other, or other such misdemeanors. You said a decade of the Rosary after each evening meal, you prayed for friends with needs, you remembered the Poor Souls in Purgatory, and you said our patented night prayer before going to bed. St. Anthony helped you find stuff. You accepted Communion as a given, a reality of the presence of Christ. We read stories from the Bible each Sunday after dinner. Your favorite story was that of the Prodigal Son, with his overjoyed father running down the road to meet him with open arms (tears running down his face).

What is the point of these memories? Simply that because you grew up Catholic—like it or not you have a Catholic identity. The same is true of my other readers. Each of you has his or her unique story of growing up Catholic. You can fight it, or try to ignore it, but you never get over it.

You are Catholic by inheritance. You are Catholic by birth, you are Catholic by baptism, and you are Catholic by custom and life experience. You are not Protestant. You are not Buddhist. If you thought you would like to drop out of the Catholic faith, what would be your new identity? You could be "Secular," but does anybody know what that means? You could slide along for awhile without really addressing the question of identity, but sooner or later you would need a coherent philosophy of life.

A philosophy of life is based on self-identity. It tries to tie together everything around us, and all of life and death, in order to make sense of it all, and give it meaning and purpose. But it's a tall order to build a new identity and a new philosophy of life, for yourself and your children—completely separated from religion—

6

that will stand the test of time and the vicissitudes of life. To paraphrase the line from the story in Genesis, "Don't give up your birthright for a mess of pottage."

While secularism is based on the premise that reality and truth are found only in the material world, and questions whether there is a God and an afterlife, Catholic teaching is based on faith that there is a loving God and Creator, a father and friend, who wants to share with us God's own life and happiness now and forever. Reality and truth also exist in this spiritual world of the infinite Creator-God, who can act in ways that are beyond our finite ability to fully understand, in a wonderful dimension of mystery and awe.

If you have faith problems and don't know what to teach your children, why not just be honest with them, taking it "bird by bird" as they ask questions, giving both points of view? This book, told as stories, is a possible resource for the Catholic view of life.

A Catholic identity is not a bad thing to hang onto, and it comes in all shapes and sizes: active and contemplative, intellectual and poetic, literal and cultural, with adaptability to your personal lifestyle if you are also willing to adapt your lifestyle to the faith. Fair enough?

Love,

Dad

Letter 2: Community and Universality

Dear Family:

At the heart of the Catholic tradition is community. Not simply fellowship, although God knows we need more of that.

Rather, the Church understands itself as a community that exemplifies Christ's words: "Where two or three are gathered in my name, there I am in their midst." Christ lives on in the community, particularly in the Mass—in the scriptures, the priest, the Consecration of the bread ad wine, the Communion, and in the assembly. The Church refers to Christ's presence in the community as the Mystical Body of Christ.

The community is a worshipping community. That's an old-fashioned word. We don't often think in those terms these days. But there is something humble and honest and generous about going to church to give back to God our gratefulness for everything God has given us—life, health, education, family, career, a home, a decent standard of living—particularly in comparison with so many others in the world. Gratefulness puts our life in perspective. "Eucharist" *means* thanksgiving.

Whether or not we find fellowship in a Catholic community, we can always find a sense of belonging.

Another defining characteristic of the Catholic faith is universality. The word "catholic" means universal, and the Catholic Church extends throughout the world.

The Catholic Church holds that Jesus Christ is the universal savior of all peoples, regardless of their religious traditions, and whether or not they know him. Those who seek the truth and do the will of God in accordance with their understanding of it will be saved (*Catechism of the Catholic Church*).

The Catholic view is all-inclusive in another sense. We take to heart the Lord's example of being there for the outcasts and the marginalized. The Church is there for the poor, the homeless, the addicted, the single mother on welfare, the victims of AIDS. She is there to find adoptive alternatives to abortion, and to counsel moth-

8

ers who have had an abortion. She has missions and relief services all over the world.

We are not an upper middle class church. As James Joyce said, "Here comes everybody!"

Love,

Dad

Letter 3: Sacramentality

Dear Family:

The Catholic faith is sacramental. Beyond the Seven Sacra-ments (discussed later) lies the principle of Sacramentality. The Catholic vision "sees" God in all things, the presence of God per-meating all of creation, the invisible made visible. God communi-cates God's spiritual presence to us through the material, not only in religious symbols, but also in persons, events, activities, nature, objects, the cosmos. God is present, and the material world and its joys and pleasures are therefore basically good, even if flawed.

Father Andrew Greeley, the priest-sociologist, likes to refer to this as the "Catholic Imagination," and in particular to the symbols, images, rituals, and holy persons of the Catholic community. In ad-dition to the sacraments themselves, "these images include the cru-cifix, the ritual of the Mass, the sign of the cross, the rosary, the stained-glass windows and statues in beautiful churches, the Sta-tions of the cross, the saints and angels, the Communion of Saints, and especially Mary, the mother of God."

Father Greeley suggests that the Catholic imagination has a propensity to a warmer, affectionate, more intimate, more living and graceful representation of ultimate reality than might others, and is more likely to think of God as a "mother," as a "spouse," and as a "friend."

The theologian Monika Hellwig emphasizes the importance of the sacramental principle in these words:

"The sacramental principle is the reality of our relationship with God. Given the confusion of the world of human experience in a history distorted by consequences of sin, we do not sponta-neously see and experience everything in relationship to God. There are moments of breakthrough, special memories and associ-ations that help. These must be treasured, reflected on, recalled, celebrated to open the awareness of the divine in our lives to ever wider circles of experience, and to learn progressively to respond to the divine..."

10

Later on we'll explore the practice of the presence of God in prayer, internally as it were, but I find this sacramental notion, the idea of God's presence in everything and everybody around us quite attractive and practical and down to earth.

In fact, one can think of Catholicism as "of the earth," physical, not vague and ethereal. The material sacramentalizes the divine in every dimension of life. The Church's rituals are replete with ashes, salt, oil, fire, water, bread, wine, and incense, each signifying God in its own way. Our churches and liturgy are surrounded by beautiful art and architecture, music, poetry and drama, all to the glory of God. We permit ourselves to rejoice in working, eating, drinking, playing; and laughing, singing, dancing, praying. It's all part of creation by a loving God who is present with us in all things.

The principle of sacramentality is a unique hallmark of the Catholic faith.

> *Wherever the Catholic sun does shine*
> *There's music and laughter and good red wine.*
> *At least I've always found it so.*
> *Benedicamus Domino!*
> -Hilaire Belloc

Love,

Dad

Letter 4: Rationality

Dear Family,

The Church doesn't believe what it believes simply because it has always believed it. Yes, the basis for belief is found in scripture and tradition, but in addition the Church has sought greater understanding of scripture and tradition through rationality, or theology.

The teachings of the Catholic Church are the products of the finest minds of the last 2,000 years. There has been a persistent effort down through the centuries to seek in the Catholic faith intellectual coherence, to understand each doctrine both within itself, and in relation to the other doctrines of the Church. Yes, human mistakes are sometimes made, but sooner or later these have or will be reformulated because of this persistent search for truth and coherence.

For example, it took the Church four centuries of prayer, religious experience, penetrating thought, intense debate, and divine guidance to sort out the dual natures of Jesus Christ, divine and human, and the nature of God as Trinity—three "Persons" in one God —and to define those teachings at the Councils of Nicea (325), Constantinople (381), Ephesus (431), and Chalcedon (451).

What is theology? Theology is "faith seeking understanding," in the words of St. Anselm of Canterbury (d.1109). It's the illumination of faith through reason, so that understanding can make the faith more real to us, and give it added dimension and practical application. Very often it is the application of the principles of philosophy to reach an understanding of faith.

Theologians, now primarily academics, are intellectual leaders and unofficial teaching authorities of the Church, and are advisors to the official Church teaching authority. Their expertise is important, not only to help us understand the faith, but also to open up new lines of interpretation of the faith in a rapidly evolving social, economic, and scientific world.
Love,

Dad

Letter 5: The Sources of Catholic Teaching

Dear Family:

Catholic teaching is based on scripture, tradition, and theology, which in turn are based on the revelation of God.

Creation itself is the revelation of God. The Bible then relates a history of meaningful encounters between God and humankind which the biblical scholar Avery Dulles summarizes as "the events of the Exodus, including the Sinai covenant (the Ten Commandments), the conquest of the Holy Land, the Exile (to Babylonia) and return, and, in the New Testament, the life, death, and resurrection of Jesus, together with the founding of the Christian Church."

The events of this history are then interpreted by inspired prophets, apostles, the Evangelists (the Evangelists are the authors of the Gospels) and the general councils and teachings of the Church.

As the incarnate Word of God, Jesus Christ is the fullness of all revelation. We see God in human form when we see Christ.

The Church understands the Bible to be written by inspired authors who produced a document which, when taken as a whole, is a reliable witness to God's revelation. It does not purport to be a scientific book, nor are all the events related necessarily historical or chronological. Individual passages may contain certain scientific or historical errors, or the literary or theological devices of the authors.

Catholics, therefore, believe the Bible to be true, but do not take it word for word. In other words, we do not agree with fundamentalism, which takes everything in the Bible word for word. Rather, the Church encourages the use of modern methods of biblical criticism, the "historical-critical" methods, which you will find in the notes. These methods assist the Church in interpreting the meaning of God's revelation in scripture.

What is tradition?

Tradition is the handing on of the faith, both in scripture and in essential teachings, and also in changeable customs and practices.

13

The liturgy—the public worship of the Church—is itself an important vehicle for handing on the tradition of the Church.

The writings of the Church Fathers are another source of tradition. They were Spirit-filled holy men of the early Church, from St. Justin Martyr (d.165) on up to Augustine (d.430).

A third ground of tradition is the "sense of the faithful" (*sensus fidelium*). Vatican II was unequivocal:

"The body of the faithful *as a whole*...cannot err in matters of belief...it manifests this unerring quality *when...it shows universal agreement in matters of faith and morals*." (Emphasis supplied.)

At rock bottom, then, faith arises from the experience of the people, even in the interpretation of revelation. The *sensus fidelium* contributes to the clarification of Christian doctrine either by protesting certain errors, or anticipating truths not yet officially taught.

Scripture, tradition and theology converge in the teaching authority of the Church, called the *magisterium*, which can be exercised in several ways.

First, what about "infallible" teaching? The Church holds that infallibility resides in the whole body of bishops when they exercise their teaching power in union with the successor of Peter, as in the great general councils of the Church, such as Nicea-Constantinople, on questions of fundamental belief. Those doctrines are called dogmas. It should be recognized that while dogmas express an authentic aspect of Christian revelation, they are historically and culturally conditioned, and may be "reformulated" to apply more aptly to new times and conditions.

The Church also holds that the Pope can speak infallibly, but only when he makes a definite pronouncement in his capacity as successor of Peter (*ex cathedra*: from the chair of Peter). This is a very limited concept, and has rarely been exercised.

However, the vast majority of the teachings of the *magisterium* do not purport to be infallible, and come in the form of papal encyclicals (letters), teaching documents from the various departments of the Vatican with the approval of the Pope, and documents produced by the various organizations of bishops. The office of Bishop itself is primarily a teaching office. It is noteworthy that the

Fathers of Vatican II (a general council) determined not to regard any of their documents as infallible.

You may be interested to know that, at least as to the ordinary teachings of the Church, there is a road well marked out for either acceptance or disagreement. The Catholic is expected to have an attitude of respectful trust for the ordinary teachings of the Church. At the same time, quoting from *The Modern Catholic Encyclopedia*: *"[The Catholic] also [has] the duty to examine critically and, if necessary, to express reservations and disagreement without rebelling against authority. Such a disagreement is legitimate and even necessary if the truth is to be discovered or better formulated."* (Emphasis supplied.)

Let me conclude this lengthy (but fun-filled) letter by returning ever-so-briefly to the subject of mystery. Despite revelation, in the deepest sense God is incomprehensible to us mortals. We are dealing with a wholly different dimension, the world of spirit, which is not confined or subject to physical laws or the limitations of human logic. Unless you are determined *a priori* to limit faith to the material world and the laws of science, you should be free to accept the proposition that faith can go beyond the limits of human understanding.

With regard to the teachings of the Church, then, please keep in mind the element of mystery.

Love,

Dad

Letter 6: What Does the Church Teach?

Dear Family:

First off, it seems that many young people are caught up in the question of what they need to believe or accept in order to be Catholic. I think that's a needless worry, and the best approach is simply to set forth the Church's basic teaching, and then in the following letter to tackle the issues of doubt and disbelief.

Christ's commandment is: Love one another as I have loved you. That means self-giving love, even self-sacrificing love. It means serving one another, as in the Lord's washing of the feet of his disciples at the Last Supper. It means forgiving one another. It means respecting the uniqueness and equal dignity of every person. It means loving with the grace of God's love.

This is the most basic teaching of the Church.

In addition, there are three articles of faith that are basic. These are found in the Nicene Creed, which we say at every Sunday Mass. A creed is a statement of belief. The Nicen Creed is based on the teachings of the general Councils of Nicea (325) and Constantinople (381). I will paraphrase these statements as follows:

(1) The Unity and Trinity of God, maker of heaven and earth, of all that is seen and unseen.

(2) The incarnation, death, and resurrection of Jesus Christ, the Son of God.

(3) The forgiveness of sin, the resurrection of the body, and eternal life with God and each other.

I would add here as basic the teachings on the Sacraments, especially the Eucharist.

In this letter I want to talk about God, creation, and the Incarnation. I'll cover the other teachings later.

God is love. God sees us individually and personally with the eyes of love, just as we see our own children with the eyes of love.

In a more philosophical vein, the Church goes on to teach that God is the fullness of being, and the essence of goodness, beauty, holiness and truth without origin and without end.

Further, the Church teaches that God is actually a community of love, one God in three Divine Persons: Father, Son, and Holy Spirit—the Holy Trinity.

How can you have three persons in one God? Obviously this is mystery of the highest order, but we can make a stab at understanding something about it.

Instead of "person" in the ordinary sense of the word, think of three ways of being, and more particularly, three ways of being in relationship to each other. Thus, God is one in "substance" (one in being), yet "Father," "Son," and "Spirit" are distinct relationships with each other. Or think of God as the Origin or Begetter, the Son as the Eternal Begotten or Expression, and the Holy Spirit as the Spirit of Love between them. St. Patrick thought the shamrock was a good way to imagine the three of them in one.

There are other ways to characterize the Trinity, but the Catechism sums it up this way:

"God's very being is love. By sending his only Son and the Spirit of Love in the fullness of time, God has revealed his innermost secret: *God himself is an eternal exchange of love, Father, Son, and Holy Spirit, and he has destined us to share in that exchange*" (emphasis supplied).

In a very real sense we are caught up into the life of the Trinity, into this eternal exchange of love, here and now and forever. As Julian of Norwich says, we are "enfolded" in love.

The world was made by God "ex nihilo" (I love that term—it has a certain theological panache), meaning "out of nothing," i.e. God loving Self into created expressions of that Self in the finite universe.

In the beginning was the Word:
The Word was in God's presence,
and the Word was God.
He was present to God in the beginning.
Through him all things came into being,
and apart from him nothing came to be.
                                    -John

Here, the Word is the Second Person of the Trinity, as the eternal expression or utterance of God. The Church tells us that their mutual expression of love co-originates eternally God's Holy Spirit —the Third Person—God's "breath." The Holy Trinity of Persons creates and sustains everything in being, constantly "breathing" life and love into all creation.

This prayer for Pentecost is familiar to all of us oldies:

Come, Holy Spirit,
Fill the hearts of your faithful,
And kindle in them the fire of your love.
Send forth your Spirit and they shall be created.
And you will renew the face of the earth.

The Catechism says that God had no reason for creating other than to share his benevolent goodness and love. The theologian Elizabeth Johnson puts it with a certain flair: "God creates in the sheer exuberance of freedom."

In short, God created humankind so that we might share God's glory (life, holiness, love) and respond gratefully and lovingly.

Genesis fills out the creation story in the form of myth, in the sense of essential truths told in a fictional, imaginative way. We don't take the story of Adam and Eve and The Fall literally. The Catholic Church does not insist on non-evolutionary "creationism," including the special creation of an original human pair.

The Church is fully aware of the possibilities of evolution as the process of development of humankind from lower species. John H. Haught, in his recent book, *God After Darwin*, argues that evolutionary biology can enrich the Church's theological views on

18

the development of humankind, and theology can likewise contribute to the science of human development.

The Church teaches that human beings are all made in the image and likeness of God, with the desire to seek fulfillment in God. This desire may be called the capacity for grace. "You have made us for yourself, O Lord, and our hearts are restless until they rest in you" (Augustine).

The fullness of grace is the gift of God's own personal life and self within us, the very life of the Trinity. This is why we were created—to share God's own life with God and each other in love.

However, to receive God's offer of grace we must exercise our free will and say "yes" to God. We must be open to God's love. God will never force our choice.

There is sinfulness in human hearts, which blocks or diminishes our ability to be open to love. Sin is of two kinds: so-called "Original Sin," and personal sin.

The story of Adam and Eve and their fall from grace attempts to describe that universal human condition the Church calls "Original Sin." Original Sin is not personal sin or fault. It is the disorder in society and ourselves resulting from the past and present sins of the world from the beginning of time, passed on from generation to generation. We are all born into this condition, with flaws in our basically good human nature, and with a tendency toward sin.

Personal sin is the sin we commit ourselves. Personal sin is any deliberate infidelity to the will of God. But we can take heart that if we slip up, God is still there for us, with God's mercy, forgiveness, loving kindness, and grace. God never gives up on us. God's love for us is eternal, absolute, benevolent, unconditional, and unchanging.

Thus the journey of life is lived out in a tension of sin and grace. The meaning of "salvation," of being ultimately "saved," is to be forgiven, healed, and made whole; and to receive an abundance of grace, sharing God's eternal life with one another.

But it cannot be overemphasized that salvation was the goal from the beginning. As stated in the Catechism, "From the beginning, God envisaged the glory of a new creation in Christ," all of us sharing with Christ in God's personal life of grace.

19

The incarnation of the Son of God was not Plan B, to save us from Adam's sin. While part of Christ's mission was to free us from the bondage of sin, the incarnation had much broader implications.

The fact is, human beings could not, by themselves, have fully responded to God's call to grace. God must effect that union for us. Richard McBrien writes: "The whole of the creative process is directed toward, and therefore culminates in, the union of the divine and the human in Jesus Christ." By god's becoming human, we have the capacity for the divine, for union with God, for grace. "Oh marvelous exchange!" sings the Church.

The meaning and purpose of life is union with God in God's own divine life, in community with each other.

Love,

Dad

Letter 7: The Problem of Belief

Dear Family:

What if I have doubt about some of the teachings of the Church? What if I actually don't believe or disagree with some of them?

There's a difference between questioning, doubt, disbelief, and dissent. Everybody has questions and doubt about one or more teachings of the Church. Faith is gift. Questioning and doubt is natural. If this whole business could be demonstrated "scientifically" then God wouldn't be God and faith wouldn't be faith. So if you have questions and doubts about certain teachings, continue questioning these teachings and try to find greater understanding.

There may be some teachings you simply don't believe or from which you actively dissent. Vatican II makes it clear that faith can't be forced. The following key statement appears in the *Declaration on Religious Freedom* of Vatican II.

"Man [sic] perceives and acknowledges the imperatives of the divine law through the mediation of conscience. In all his activity a man is bound to follow his conscience faithfully, in order that he may come to God, for whom he was created. It follows that he is not to be forced to act in a manner contrary to his conscience."

In other words, you must believe only what you *can believe* in good conscience after a good faith effort to understand. *You are Catholic if you want to be Catholic, and want to believe and participate as best you can.* You are seeking the truth, or you wouldn't be reading this book. I believe that seekers of good will, sincere heart, and honest intellect can find a home in the Church, in their own way.

So, I think you can relax a little about what and how you believe and what and how you don't believe. It will sort itself out in time if you let yourself be an active Catholic in the sense of attending Mass whenever you can, and, if you have a family, saying simple prayers together at home.

21

The other problem with faith I'd like to talk about in this letter is the problem of evil.

The problem of evil is not so much a Catholic issue (although it has consumed the thought of many Catholic theologians) as it is a question of the existence of God. How do you handle it, because I'm sure you've heard the question from your agnostic friends: "If you believe in God who is good, how can this God allow so much evil to happen?"

We honestly don't know. But we don't start with the problem of the evil we can't understand; rather, we start with the God we think we do know. We do believe in a God who is good. We do believe in a God we can trust. Then we ask ourselves: is there something about the way God found it good to create a world that is constantly changing and evolving, not static—and a humankind that is fleshly, not spiritual, and endowed with free will. All this seems to require that we be created as fragile organic beings vulnerable to natural disaster, and to sin, disease, and death. But also capable of growth and love.

Whatever the reason, the Church takes the position that God does not intend suffering and loss, but for some reason permits it to occur. And that God knows that no evil will finally win out. Rather, good will triumph over all evil. We take solace in the words of St. Paul: "We know that God makes all things work together for the good of those who love God," and of Julian of Norwich: "But all shall be well, and all shall be well, and all manner of thing shall be well."

We do know this much from our own experience: Suffering and loss and death are not moral evil. Through our own will, intention, and prayer, aided by the grace of God, suffering and loss and death can be occasions and instruments of transforming love and redeeming gain.

For many Catholics, suffering is made easier to bear when we remember that God himself suffered and died for us, and, in some mysterious way, still suffers in solidarity with us, with infinite compassion, and we in solidarity with God.

Love,
Dad

Letter 8: The Church and Sex

Dear Family:

Do you remember those lines from William Blake?

And priests in black gowns
Were walking their rounds,
And binding with briers
My joys and desires

I used to think that was so neat. And of course that sums up the opinion of your generation about the Catholic Church and sex. Why is that? Surely no one is going to blame the Church for its age-old teaching that sex is for marriage. That injunction may be observed in the breach these days, but it's good law, and nothing to badmouth the Church about.

The Church has long held that in general the sexual act must be both unitive (loving) and procreative (open to bearing children), based on natural law. The Church sees heterosexual marriage and a secure family home as the sole context for sexual love and the pro-creation and nurturing of life. That's it in a nutshell. I am not competent to advise young people on specific sexual standards in specific situations.

But I can talk about contraception and abortion, and how the co-existence of these subjects in Catholic teaching contributes to the notion of young adults that the Church is against sex.

The encyclical *Humanae Vitae (1968)* upheld the traditional teaching of the Church that each and every marriage act must remain open to the transmission of life, and that artificial contraception is objectively wrong.

This conclusion was based on the "inseparable link" between the unitive and procreative functions of the marriage act. In support of such a link the encyclical refers to the tradition of the Church and also to natural law.

The majority of the special papal commission that had studied the matter had recommended a change in the tradition of teaching.

The majority held "that the morality of sexual acts between married people takes its meaning first of all and specifically from the ordering of their actions in a fruitful married life. It does not then depend upon the fecundity of each and every particular act." However, after much agony of conscience, Pope Paul VI issued the encyclical.

There is a widespread lack of acceptance of this Church teaching, even among practicing Catholics. However, other Catholics do follow the traditional teaching of the Church, some using the natural family planning method which is recommended by the Church.

The Church also teaches that abortion is wrong. But here I believe that most Catholics agree.

I recognize that others take a different view, and I am sensitive to all the ramifications of unwanted pregnancies and their real life consequences.

I say this because in my opinion we are dealing with the question of life and death of human beings. If that is true, then the problem of unwanted pregnancies must, in the very nature of things, take second place.

The Catholic Church holds that, while the human body may have been in part the product of evolution, the infusion of the human soul is the direct creation of God resulting in an individual, personal, and unique human life. In a sense, the soul is the "substantial principle" of the person, i.e. That which makes us what we are and who we are. From then on the soul is immortal.

While some theologians suggest the possibility that the human person does not exist until 14 days after conception (see note), the Church raises the presumption that the fertilized egg becomes a human being at the moment of conception.

Biology tells us that from the beginning the growth and development of the embryo and fetus is a continuum leading to viability and full term. At the end of the third week the heart begins to beat and the blood begins to circulate through the primitive vascular system. Within a month the mother knows or suspects she is pregnant. Most abortions occur after that. In the Catholic view, which is

24

consistent with biology, there is no question the embryo is a human being within a month.

My point to young adult Catholics is this: disagree if you must, but don't apologize for the Church's position. It is logical, humane, and *life-giving*. The Church does not deserve disdain on this issue.

Roe v. Wade itself is not a model of thorough fact-finding and high legal principles based on solid legal precedent, such as can provide one with moral comfort. The decision does not even define human being when it makes the artificial distinction between the first trimester and the second trimester.

The burden of proof in this entire controversy is on those who advocate abortion. Ask them to explain at what point in the continuum human life begins. And do not let the issue of abortion become confused with the issue of contraception.

I believe the ambivalence of some young Catholics on abortion is due not so much to acceptance of abortion itself, but rather to sympathy with those who espouse abortion or who have an unwanted pregnancy and actually have an abortion. There is also a fear of being thought judgmental or not politically correct, which should have nothing to do with it. The Church itself offers care and compassion to those who may suffer from the aftermath of abortion.

Therefore I urge you to develop a good understanding of this issue so that you know your position and can state it clearly.

Love,

Dad

Letter 9: The Church and Women

Dear Family:

A significant number of young people, mostly women, are put off by the fact the Church is a male-dominated institution from the top down.

I can recite many improvements in the status of women in the Church in recent years: female altar servers, women lectors and Eucharist ministers, women preachers, women administrators of parishes where there is no priest, women theologians, the use of inclusive language. In point of fact, women are running most parishes, and many of the departments in the dioceses. But I think the big issue for some is how come no women priests?

Pope John Paul II declared in his 1994 apostolic letter *Ordinatio Sacerdotalis* that the Church as no *authority* to confer priestly ordination on women. It was Jesus Christ who founded the priesthood, and he chose only men, even though he was surrounded by women in his ministry.

Nevertheless, debate within the Church continues, including arguments in favor of women priests from the Canon Law Society of America, the Catholic Theological Society of America, and the Leadership Council of Women Religious. Basically they argued for the equality of women, that there is nothing in sacred scripture which positively excludes the ordination of women, and that the original choice of males was cultural. In short, they respectfully disagreed with the Pope's position and felt that it lacked convincing proof or argument.

Be that as it may, the Pope has spoken on this issue, and doubtless the Church will abide by his decision for a good while into the future.

There is nothing in scripture that is an impediment to a married clergy. The Apostles were family men. During the first ten centuries of the Church's existence the custom or rule regarding celibacy varied widely at various times and places

In the twelfth century, partly under the influence of monasticism, and partly to prevent inheritance of Church property going outside the Church, the Church developed a general rule of celibacy. But even now, some Catholic rites permit marriage before ordination, and a growing number of exceptions are being made for married clergy entering the Church from other Christian denominations.

It is my understanding that the Church regards this as a policy issue and can change this whenever it so decides.

However the question of a married clergy may go, there will still be an option available for celibacy. Celibacy is a profound sign of personal sacrifice and total dedication to God. Jesus said, "Not everyone can accept this teaching, only those to whom it is given to do so." The Church would be a poorer place without these dedicated men and women who have served us so faithfully all these centuries, and who will continue to do so in the future.

Love,

Dad

Letter 10: The Life of Jesus

Dear Family:

I want to tell the story of the life of Jesus of Nazareth, up to the time of his death, knowing full well that the story comes to us filtered through the light of faith as found in the Gospels.

Jesus of Nazareth was a real human person who walked the land of Galilee 2,000 years ago. See the notes for collateral ancient references to his existence. Ever since I started spending these summer sessions with your mother and her colleagues at the archaeological dig at Bethsaida on the Sea of Galilee I feel I've come to know this man better as a real, human person.

Jesus of Nazareth was born no later than 4 B.C., when Herod the Great died. He was born in Bethlehem. His mother, Mary, daughter of Anne and the priest Joachim, possibly was born in Jerusalem, but most likely was born in Nazareth. The Church reverences her birthplace as the church of St. Anne on the Via Dolorosa in Jerusalem.

Joseph was born in either Nazareth or Bethlehem, but lived in Nazareth as an adult. Nazareth is in the region of Galilee in northern Palestine, with the Sea of Galilee in its heart.

Catholic tradition believes that the "brothers and sisters" of Jesus mentioned in the Gospels were cousins of Jesus—his extended family.

There is another possibility that Joseph could have been a widower with the six mentioned children. Either way, Jesus would have grown up surrounded by a large family.

The Church teaches both the "immaculate conception" of Mary, and the virgin birth of Jesus. These are two entirely different matters related to Mary.

Because Mary was destined to become the human mother of God, by the gift of God Mary was free of "original sin" and was "full of grace" (the divine life) from the moment of her natural conception by her mother, Anne.

The Church not only teaches the virgin birth of Jesus, but also that thereafter Mary remained a virgin. Mary said "yes" to the angel who revealed her becoming the human mother of God by the power of the Holy Spirit. The Church teaches that God is the father of the God-man Jesus.

Mary herself asked, "How can this be?" The angel in effect replied, "Why not? With God all things are possible."

The fundamental doctrine is that Jesus did not *become* one with God as time went on: *Jesus was one with God from the moment of his conception.* Jesus was the Son of God, the Word made flesh.

Jesus grew up with his family at Nazareth in Galilee. His life is hidden from us until about the age of 32 or later (this age, and the dates given hereafter, are not certain, but are agreed upon as approximate by most scholars). He is referred to in the Gospels as "the carpenter's son," very likely working with Joseph until the latter's death.

Since archeology shows that Nazareth was a village of only about 150 people, Jesus may have worked in the construction of nearby Sepphoris, the new capital of Herod Antipas, ruler of Galilee. Sepphoris was a Hellenized city (i.e. influenced by the culture of the earlier Greek occupation) and it is interesting to speculate on how much of the Greek culture Jesus assimilated, from learning Greek to seeing Greek plays.

However he spent those years, Jesus had totally absorbed his country background, and all those stored images emerge time and again in his discourses, with consummate artistry: "Who among you, if he has a hundred sheep and loses one of them, does not leave the ninety-nine to find the one who is lost?" "Consider the lilies of the field, neither do they sow nor do they spin, yet I tell you Solomon in all his glory was not arrayed as one of these."

In the year 28 A.D., Jesus began his public ministry, which lasted about 2 ½ years until his death in Jerusalem on April 6, 30 A.D. Most of this time was spent in Galilee and around the Sea of Galilee, with occasional journeys to Jerusalem for the special feasts, and two or three forays into Gentile territory. Here is a sketch of Jesus' ministry in Galilee (following the outline prepared by Father Bargil Pixner):

- Jesus was baptized by his cousin John in the early winter of 28 in the lower Jordan near Jericho. In John's company he found his original disciples, from the fishing town of Bethsaida on the northeast shore of the Sea of Galilee. He made his headquarters in Capernaum on the Sea of Galilee, with Peter and the other disciples (the site of Peter's house is identified today). Jesus preached and healed for an extended period in the area known to scholars as the "Evangelical Triangle" of Capernaum, Bethsaida, and Korazin, and beyond.

- At the heart of Jesus' preaching was his proclamation that the Kingdom of God was at hand. *The Kingdom of God is like a metaphor for the transforming presence and power of God in ourselves, our lives, and our society—here, now, in the future, and at the end of time.*

- Tradition has the First Feeding of the Multitude occurring on the west side of the lake at Tabgha. This miraculous event symbolized the bringing of God's life and salvation to the Israelites. The excited crowd wanted to make Jesus king, thereby endangering his life under the watchful eye of Herod at nearby Tiberias (who had already executed John).

- Jesus therefore retreated with his disciples for a time to the Gentile territory of Phoenicia, where he healed the child of a Gentile woman, after her insistent pleadings. Up to that point Jesus had understood his mission to be to the Israelites alone, but the faith of this woman touched him deeply, and may have been instrumental in causing him to open up his mission to include the Gentiles.

- So from there he went to the Gentiles in the Decapolis, a Hellenized region on the east side of the lake, where he accomplished the Second Feeding of the Multitude, which symbolized the bringing of God's life and salvation to the Gentiles, and to the rest of the world. These feedings of the multitudes foretold the later establishment of the Eucharist.

- Jesus was back in Capernaum by the fall of 29. Since the beginning of his public life he had experienced rising tensions with certain of the Pharisees, a conservative and powerful Jewish religious party, because of his independent interpretation of the law (for example, he excoriated the Pharisees for their complaint that he healed on the Sabbath) and by his claim to forgive sin ("Which is easier, to say 'arise and walk' or to say 'your sins are forgiven'"), which put him on an equal footing with God.

- Now the conflict reached a climax with Jesus' "Bread of Life" discourse in the synagogue at Capernaum: "Unless you eat my flesh and drink my blood you will not have life in you." The Pharisees turned away from him at this, as did many of his own followers.

- In general, at this point in time Jesus' mission to the Israelites was failing, even as his appeal to the Gentiles was gaining. The Israelite crowds loved the healing and the miracles, but only a few believed in him and his message. We wonder why. Jesus may have realized that only by his death could he accomplish his mission of bringing about more fully the Kingdom of God.

- Even his own Twelve thought he would be a political Messiah, and lead a movement to rid Israel of the Romans. So Jesus took them on a long (35 mile) journey of instruction up to Caesarea Philippi, during which he prepared them for his imminent death. He then took Peter, James, and John to the high mountain (probably Mt. Hermon), where he was transfigured before them, a mystical experience that would strengthen them for the ordeal to come.

- Upon his return to Capernaum he received a warning from certain Pharisees, friendly or unfriendly, that Herod was out to kill him. His reply was "Go tell that fox..." I will leave when my work is finished.

- In March, 30, Jesus received word that his friend Lazarus was deathly ill at Bethany near Jerusalem, so Jesus went up to Jerusalem, to the raising of Lazarus, and to prepare for his own death

---

The present day archaeological dig at Bethsaida, on the Sea of Galilee, is the one sure place in Galilee, if not in all Israel, that you can walk down a street where you know that Jesus actually walked.

Bethsaida was lost for nearly 2,000 years, and everything uncovered on the top later is first century.

What did Jesus know about himself? The consensus of modern theology is that Jesus operated primarily out of his human nature. But he knew he had an intimate, profound and continuous relationship with the Father; and he knew that he had a special mission to bring about salvation through the Kingdom of God, with the special knowledge, authority, and power to carry it through.

What was he like? The Gospels never describe him physically. Maybe it's just as well—he has to be a universal figure for us today.

But he certainly wasn't the Wimp in the White Robe, or the Man Who Never Smiled. That Jesus could not be human.

In fact here was a man who lived outdoors and had the strength and vitality of a construction worker; a man who got very angry when he saw people being unjustly pushed around by authority; a man who grew up as a Jewish teenager, dancing and laughing and singing, and who as an adult loved to share meals with people and drink a little wine, rounding up all the strays and outcasts; a man who could rouse huge crowds with his confident and charismatic voice; a man who could weep over Jerusalem, and for his dear friend Lazarus.

This man had to have been warm-hearted and smiling and outgoing and caring, or those simple people of Capernaum would never have had the nerve to press around him until he had no time to eat or rest, as he touched them and healed them, touched and healed. Here was a man who was fully human.

Yet he had the gravitas, the edge, and the challenge of a prophet. He didn't mince words about what God expected. If he was kind to sinners, he also braced them to shape up. If he reached out to befriend the Pharisees, he also gave no quarter in those quick Jewish-style debates with their teachers and lawyers. In the end, he faced down Pontius Pilate. The man was tough, and he was nobody's fool.

32

But also, he had a presence and a power beyond the human. Jesus cured the medically incurable. He performed "mighty works" outside the course of nature. He spoke with a seeming God-given authority. He called upon his Father as an intimate. He presumed to forgive sins. Human, yes, but no ordinary human.

What was his message? Here is Jesus' own description of his mission, given in his hometown synagogue at Nazareth, as reported in the Gospel of Luke"

The spirit of the Lord is upon me;
Therefore he has anointed me.
He has sent me to bring glad tidings to the poor,
To proclaim liberty to captives,
Recovery of sight to the blind and release to prisoners,
To announce a year of favor from the Lord.

The Kingdom of God is not about sweetness and light. Jesus was not "meek and mild." Jesus was a revolutionary. Not a political revolutionary, but a revolutionary of the religious, moral, and economic order. He wanted to turn the values of the world upside down with love. Eventually he paid for it with his life.

Jesus proclaimed the Kingdom of God in those sayings that have been collected as the Sermon on the Mount. At the heart of those sayings are the Beatitudes.

Blessed are the poor in spirit, for theirs is the kingdom of God.
Those conscious of the limitations of human life, and aware of their need for God, will find fulfillment.
Blessed are those who hunger and thirst for righteousness...
Those who have this right relationship with God will be filled.
Blessed are the merciful...
Those who are compassionate will receive compassion.
Blessed are the single-hearted...
Those who single-heartedly seek God will know the presence of God.

Blessed are the peacemakers...

Those who reconcile conflict will be called the children of God.

These and other beatitudes are the spiritual charter of the Kingdom of God.

And then there was Jesus the storyteller. Is there a more tender story in all literature than the parable of the Prodigal Son? "While he was still a long way off, his father caught sight of him and was deeply moved. He ran out to meet him, threw his arms around his neck, and kissed him." (I used to throw in "with tears running down his cheeks".)

Pope John Paul II treats this story with great sensitivity in his Encyclical *Dives in Misericordia* (Rich in Mercy) as the story of God's true mercy. The Father's love goes beyond forgiveness. He puts a robe on his son, and kills the fatted calf. His son is found, restored to value, and receives back the dignity that he once had. His lost innocence is restored. What message can be more heartening to those who feel they have messed up their lives beyond hope, beyond self-respect? If there is one, clear, human thing that Jesus stands for it is the dignity of the individual human person no matter what.

There is another human thing that Jesus clearly stands for, and it is brought out in his second-best story, the Good Samaritan. Active compassion. We don't pass by. We stop. We give of our time and our substance. We give of ourselves. Does it matter? It's everything. It's the separation of the sheep from the goats on judgment day. Who is our neighbor? Everybody.

There are one or two other things to mention before ending this long letter. Jesus healed. And Jesus performed "mighty works" (miracles). These are "signs" of the Kingdom.

Jesus healed because he is a man of compassion, and God is a God of compassion, and the Kingdom is about compassion, salvation, and the healing of body and soul. We may not understand why suffering exists, but we can know by the example of Jesus' healing ministry that God cannot abide suffering for itself. However, he surely knows all about it. He voluntarily took it upon himself in the end.

The Catholic Church does not back down from the existence of miracles in Jesus' ministry, despite the Enlightenment, modern science, and skeptics and all that. It all depends upon your *a priori* assumptions about the existence and power of God.

The Church teaches that Jesus performed miracles as signs of God's power and the overcoming of evil. However, there is a wide spectrum of views among theologians as to what certain miracle stories mean, from simple acceptance in a fundamentalist sense, to rejection of some as hyperbole.

To quote Richard McBrien, "Certain events apparently did take place, and they were taken, by friend and foe alike, as marvelous in their own right. The sick were cured, for example. Jesus' enemies did not challenge the fact of the cure but the propriety of curing on the Sabbath."

On the other hand, did Jesus really walk on the water to calm the waves after a sudden storm? Well, if he could raise Lazarus, maybe he did and maybe he didn't. It's a lively story that makes a point about personal faith in him.

To sum it up: Catholics believe that Jesus of Nazareth was the Son of God, the Word of God become incarnate for our salvation. The letter of John says it best.

> *What was from the beginning,*
> *What we have heard,*
> *What we have seen with our eyes,*
> *What we looked upon*
> *And touched with our own hands*
> *Concerns the Word of life...*
> *We proclaim to you the eternal life*
> *That was with the Father*
> *And was made visible to us*

Love,

Dad

Letter 11: The Jesus of Faith

Dear Family:

I said in an earlier letter the Church teaches that Jesus came for our salvation, and defined salvation to be ultimately forgiven, healed and made whole, to receive the abundance of grace, and to be eternally united with God and one another. I also said that the Church teaches that God would have become man to help us to reach this goal of abundant life regardless of "the sin of Adam" or our personal sin.

Yet we know that the Church and the Eucharistic liturgy place great emphasis on the passion and death of Jesus as an essential part of our salvation. The Church understands this as our "redemption" (L. *redemptio*, "buying back") by Jesus from the bondage of sin so that we might be open to the grace of the resurrection. More on this below. But first we need to set the stage.

We've seen that Jesus had challenged and scandalized the leaders of his own Jewish faith with his independent interpretation of the Law, and with his claim to forgive sin which put him on an equal footing with God. When he left Galilee under threat from Herod Antipas, who considered him a troublemaker, and went up to Jerusalem, the religious authorities became greatly concerned that Jesus could jeopardize the safety of Jews under the Roman yoke, because Jesus could be the focus for insurrection among the large crowds gathered in Jerusalem for the Passover feast. It was decided, as Caiphas the High Priest remarked, that it was better to have one man die than to have the whole nation destroyed.

And so the Passion narrative begins with the Last Supper.

It appears from the Gospel of John that Jesus foretold the Last Supper and the Eucharist in his "Bread of Life" sermon at Capernaum shortly after the feeding of the multitude (itself a sign of the Eucharist).

I myself am the living bread
come down from heaven.

36

If anyone eats this bread
he shall live forever;
the bread I will give
is my flesh [my body], for the life of the world...
For my flesh is real food
and my blood real drink.

The original Greek makes it clear that these words were meant literally. His listeners understood them literally. "At this the Jews quarreled among themselves, saying, 'How can he give us his flesh to eat?' Thereupon Jesus said to them: 'If you do not eat the flesh of the Son of Man and drink his blood, you have no life in you'... From this time on many of his disciples broke away and would not remain in his company any longer. Jesus then said to the Twelve, 'Do you want to leave me too?' Simon Peter answered him, 'Lord, to whom shall we go? You have the words of eternal life.'"

At the Last Supper Jesus instituted the Eucharist with similar words, as set forth in Eucharist Prayer I of the missal:

"He broke the bread
gave it to his disciples, and said:
Take this, all of you, and eat it:
this is my body
which will be given up for you.
...He took the cup...
gave the cup to his disciples, and said:
Take this, all of you, and drink from it:
this is the cup of my blood,
the blood of the new and everlasting covenant.
It will be shed for you and for all
so that sins may be forgiven.
Do this in memory of me."

What does this mean? The Church teaches that the institution of the Eucharist at the Last Supper established a new covenant in love between God and all of his people, to enhance the old covenant in law between God and his chosen people, the Jewish nation. The old covenant was, "I will be your God and you will be my people." The new covenant is the binding together of the community in Christ, and the sharing of God's own life with us and with each other—the life of grace. "I will live in you and you in me." We share this life with God and each other in a special way in the Eucharist by receiving ritually Christ's body and blood within us.

At the Last Supper Jesus actualized and made present for all time his sacrificial death, his resurrection, and his new life—*in his own person, in the appearance of bread and wine.* This *is* my body [myself]. This *is* the cup of my blood [my life]. This *is* the new and everlasting covenant: *"I will live in you and you in me."* this was no sentimental memorial. In the light of what happened the next day, this was very real.

> *For our sake he was crucified*
> *under Pontius Pilate;*
> *he suffered, died, and was buried.*
>   -The Nicene Creed

Death by crucifixion was unbelievably horrible and cruel, devised by the Romans to extract the last breath of pain and shame from the helpless victim. It was a slow death by suffocation—public, naked, pierced by nails.

Why did Jesus have to suffer? Catholic tradition has it that the humiliation and terrible suffering of Jesus were all part of his passionate love for us, which takes away our sins and saves us. Jesus "suffered for us." But this belief can easily lead us to the false idea that Jesus was punished for our sins, that his suffering paid for us a debt of sin that we owed to a righteous Father, and that his suffering balanced the scales of divine justice. That part of tradition is plain wrong and destructive, and gives us a distorted image of God.

The tradition of Christ's "satisfaction" for our sins was taken up by Anselm of Canterbury (d.1109), later reinforced by Thomas Aquinas in the thirteenth century, and became part of the controversies of the Reformation, so that Catholics and Protestants alike

38

adhered to some version of the tradition. But now the Church understands differently. Jesus' suffering was not willed but only permitted by God, and was an act of pure, sacrificial love.

As discussed earlier, we don't fully understand suffering. But we can understand enough to know that Jesus suffered *for us*, in that for our sake he bore the suffering that was thrust upon him before his death.

Why did Jesus have to die? Jesus' words at the Last Supper are "so that sins may be forgiven." Modern theology interprets this to mean that Jesus' death was a free gift of his entire existence to a loving Father on behalf of all humankind (an at-one-ment/atonement). *By this act, as God-man, Jesus lovingly assumed the sin and guilt of the world, and reconciled us sinners with God. He set us free of our sin, so that we could be open to the grace of the resurrection.*

The Church keeps the image of the crucifix before us to demonstrate Christ's solidarity with us in our own suffering, and to remind us of the cost and depth of Christ's love for us.

> *On the third day he rose again*
> *in fulfillment of the Scriptures;*
> *he ascended into heaven*
> *and is seated at the right hand of the Father.*
> -The Nicene Creed

While the Church reserves her most poignant devotion to Jesus' dying on Good Friday, the Church explodes with joy for the Risen Lord of Easter Sunday. "He is not here! He has gone before you into Galilee. Christ is risen!"

There is little question that the crucifixion is an historical fact. What about the resurrection? Or as the question is usually put, was there an empty tomb? The short answer is if the tomb has been intact it would have been impossible to propose the resurrection story in the first place. The question is not the empty tomb, but rather what happened to Jesus' body? Was it stolen? Was it eaten by dogs (a theory of one of our current skeptics)?

Unless one decides to throw out completely the witness of the New Testament scriptures; the faith and courage, boldness and enthusiasm of the early Church; two thousand years of history in which countless generations believed and still believe they have personally encountered and experienced the Risen Lord; and the witness of the countless martyrs who have been willing to die for him ("martyr" means witness)—it would seem reasonable to accept the resurrection as a fact. *Something real happened.*

As "historical" fact? More likely a "metahistorical" fact. To quote Richard McBrien: "It is transhistorical, or metahistorical, in the sense that it refers to an event that took place on the other side of death and, therefore, which lies beyond the confines of time and space."

The traditional assurance of the resurrection lies in the appearances of Jesus after his death. St. Paul quotes the accounts of these appearances, which accounts go back to within a few years of the crucifixion. "...He appeared to Cephas, then to the twelve. Then he appeared to more than five hundred brethren at one time, most of whom are still alive... Then he appeared to James, then to all the apostles." Paul concludes: "Last of all, as to one untimely born, he appeared also to me," a reference to his encounter with the Lord on the way to Damascus.

The "appearance" stories of the Gospels round out and humanize this sparse account: Mary Magdalen first thinking he was the gardener until he said her name and she immediately clung to him; the two disciples encountering him on the way to Emmaus, "their hearts burning" as he opened their eyes to the scriptures foretelling his passion, and recognizing him "in the breaking of the bread"; the story of doubting Thomas, who is ourselves; Peter seeing Jesus on the shore of the lake cooking breakfast, and impulsively jumping overboard to go to him; and the many other stories. These stories have the ring of truth because of their naturalness and simplicity.

Who is the Risen Christ? He is the same human Jesus we have come to know, but who is now "glorified." His death has transformed him into the fullness of his human and divine natures, with the glory he had with the Father from the beginning. He is "Our

Lord." He is not simply Jesus resuscitated to his former mortal life, but rather he is Jesus resurrected to a new life. He has passed into a new dimension of matter, time and space as a glorified body—into a new mode of existence, which he has promised we will share with him at our own resurrection.

But what does the resurrection mean to us, here and now, personally? *Jesus' death and resurrection were one event at the same point in time. When Jesus offered up his entire human and divine existence to the Father at his death, he did it on our behalf. In that same act he definitively accepted on our behalf and for all time God's offer of grace—God's own life—the life that God has been waiting to give us from the beginning of creation. This "one brief shining moment" was the climax of God's plan of salvation.*

We too, and all generations until the end of time, can now accept grace by accepting the divinizing presence of God, and by allowing this gracious gift from our Lord to become deeper within is through our prayer life, by our attendance at Mass and reception of the Eucharist, and by self-giving love to others.

At the same moment of his resurrection came his "Ascension" and the sending of the Holy Spirit, which continued into Pentecost, and is still continuing until the end of time.

Despite the Gospel stories of Jesus literally being raised up to heaven at the Ascension, it's my own understanding that after his resurrection and the period of his appearances Jesus simply made a farewell to his disciples and disappeared from sight. Why? So that the Holy Spirit could multiply his presence in each of us individually, in the Church, and in the whole world as the one life-giving Spirit of grace.

Jesus had promised that he would not "leave us orphans," but that the Father and he would send the Holy Spirit in Jesus' "name." This means that the Spirit was to be sent to continue his presence and saving work among us.

The Church celebrates this event at Pentecost, the birthday of the Church, when the Holy Spirit arrived in power to inspire and strengthen, and to give courage and enthusiasm to the Apostles and disciples in order for them to carry out their mission of spreading the Gospel, the "Good News" of Jesus Christ, to the ends of the earth.

The Creed and the liturgy recite that Jesus is "seated at the right hand of the Father," which seems to contradict his promise, "know that I will be with you always, even to the end of the world." This figure of speech simply reflects the ancient image of God in the "heavens," seated on a throne, with Jesus resuming his place of honor with the Father in the glory he had from the beginning.

The fundamental, radical meaning of "the Good News" is that by the passion, death, and resurrection of Jesus Christ, through the Holy Spirit, we are now fully empowered to live the life of grace— to share in God's life—both here on earth and in the life to ccome.

Love,

Dad

Letter 12: The Jesus of the Eucharist

Dear Family:

First, some definitions. The word "Mass" comes from the words of dismissal in the old Roman rite ("*ite, missa est*"). It is the common name for the Eucharist (Gk., "thanksgiving"). "Eucharist" means both the sacrament of the Body and Blood of Christ and the entire liturgy and ritual in which the sacrament is celebrated—the entire Mass. A "liturgy" is a public worship service of the Church. "Ritual" is an established pattern of words, symbols and actions that interprets and expresses reality, often with drama and beauty.

The liturgy and ritual of the Mass began to take its present form in the second century, based on the general form of the Hebrew liturgy. Elements of Hebrew liturgy are still evident at Mass in the readings from the Old Testament, the singing of the Responsorial Psalm, and the prayers at the Presentation of the Gifts.

The earliest Eucharist prayer dates from the third century. At some point there was included its touching memorial to the martyrs: "Ignatius, Alexander, Marcellinus, Peter, Felicity, Perpetua, Agatha, Lucy, Agnes, Cecilia, Anastasia," now never to be forgotten.

The magnificent Gloria dates from the fourth century.

The Mass is divided into the Liturgy of the Word and the Liturgy of the Eucharist.

The Liturgy of the Word, in the first part of the Mass, proclaims the word of God through the scriptures, on Sundays a reading from the Old Testament, an Apostolic letter (usually a letter of St. Paul), and the Gospel. The Church teaches that Christ is present to us in these readings, and urges us to consider that he is speaking to each of us personally. The homily by the priest is usually an interpretation of these scriptures.

The Liturgy of the Word is followed by the Liturgy of the Eucharist. However, the entire liturgy is essentially indivisible. It is the story of salvation leading up to a three-fold event: (1) the "re-presentation" of the Last Supper as the sacrament of Christ's death, resurrection, and new life; (2) our offering of this sacrament to the

43

Father in thanksgiving and praise: (3) our sharing together this sacrament in Communion.

Over the centuries Catholic tradition has surrounded the Mass with all those symbols and customs we hold dear: the crucifix (the cost of love); the altar (God's sacrificial table); the tabernacle (going back to the Ark of the Covenant); the sanctuary lamp (the Hebrew symbol for Moses' Burning Bush); the table of votive candles (people of every religion have always lit candles for their deceased, and their prayer intentions); the altar candles (God as Light); the incense (the ancient symbol of all religions for the presence of the sacred); the Stations of the Cross; the statues and stained glass windows (they taught the medieval church when people couldn't read); the beauty of the church itself (we believe in a God who loves beauty).

The Eucharist is the preeminent sacrament of the Catholic Church, the "breaking of the bread." The Eucharist is the visible sign of the founding of the Church through the Twelve at the Last Supper; the visible sign of Christ's presence among us as "Church"; the visible sign of his sacrificial (self-giving) death; and the visible sign of our sacred banquet with the Risen, glorified Jesus, now and to the end of time. We don't focus exclusively on the presence of Christ in the bread and wine itself, but rather on his total presence among us.

Blessed are you, Lord, God of all creation. Through your goodness we have this bread to offer, which earth has given and human hands have made. It will become for us the bread of life.

At the Preparation of the Gifts, along with these gifts of bread and wine, we offer ourselves—our blessings and sufferings, our work, our hopes—to be transformed by the Eucharist.

After the commencement of the Eucharist prayer we come immediately to the Consecration by the priest:

This is my body, which will be given up for you. This is the cup of my blood, the blood of the new and everlasting covenant. It will be shed for you and for all so that sins may be forgiven. Do this in memory of me.

At the consecration, Jesus' whole existence is made present in the definitive event of his life—the moment of his death when he gave up his body and shed his blood in order to open the way to grace. The bread and wine are transformed into the Body and Blood of Jesus through the power of the Holy Spirit. Jesus' sacrifice is then offered to the Father by the priest and by the entire community in a celebration of praise and thanksgiving.

After the consecration, the whole Church, both living and dead, are joined in the Eucharist prayer, reminding us that this celebration reaches out beyond space and time to include all our loved ones in the Communion of Saints.

Lord, I am not worthy to receive you, but only say the word and I shall be healed.

Jesus now completes the celebration of his self-giving love by giving us himself in the form of Bread and Wine. This is intimate physical union with God in a moment of pure grace—the ultimate sacrament.

Richard McBrien sums up the Eucharist beautifully:

"Through the Eucharist, Jesus invites us to a table fellowship that is in anticipation of the heavenly banquet itself, one that is open to everyone: outcasts, tax-collectors, and anyone else marginalized by a respectable society. In celebrating the Eucharist, we take on the mind and heart of Jesus himself, opening ourselves, as he did, to everyone without exception and committing ourselves to the creation of a world where no one is excluded from the table. When Jesus said 'Do this in memory of me,' he was asking us not only to repeat the celebration of the Eucharist but also to fulfill the missionary mandate implied in the celebration."

In other words, "Do this in memory of me" means not only re-enacting the Eucharistic celebration, but also imitating Christ's self-giving love in our own lives.

45

Go in peace to love and serve the Lord and each other.

And so we go forth to witness and to serve.

Love,

Dad

Letter 13: Why go to Mass?

Dear Family:

It seems appropriate after the previous letter on the Eucharist to talk about going to Mass. If you have been avoiding going to Mass you probably felt you had good reasons. I can guess at some of them. Perhaps problems with belief in general. Perhaps anger with the Church's stance on sex and gender. I've tried to address those problems in earlier letters. Or maybe you just want to preserve "family values" without disrupting the weekend with Mass.

But there may be a more direct problem about the Mass itself —difficulty understanding or accepting the meaning of the Eucharist as I have described it. Here I can only make it personal. In the end we all have to make personal what the Eucharist means to us.

To me, the Eucharist is the presence of Christ, here and now. I see the re-presentation of the Last Supper. "This *is* my body." "This *is* the cup of my blood." "*Do this* in memory of me."

I think of these words as real. I think at the Last Super they were real. I always have.

But to what end? I think to make *present* for all time the saving death, resurrection, and new life of Christ. By "saving" I mean the transformation of Christ, which opened our lives to grace, and continues to do so by transforming *us* now.

So that when I receive communion, I think I am taking the life of Christ—grace—within me. In union with everyone else who happens to be in church, and in union with a lot of other people in the world.

For me, the Eucharist is an extraordinary event. I go to Mass because it's important. But if I didn't have this kind of belief—if I thought the Eucharist were a symbolic event—I would still go because it's important. It's a way to give back to God our entire lives —our gifts, blessings, work, sufferings, love—in thanksgiving, in the form of the bread and wine we bring up at the offertory. We offer these to God in union with Christ's offering of his entire life as bread and wine at the Last Supper. We pray that God will accept these offerings and be with us in our daily lives. When we receive communion it's sharing a meal with each other, and even in this symbolic sense it's also sharing a meal with God.

It would seem there's a need for something more important than we are in our lives, or we become ingrown upon ourselves and our search for career fulfillment, pleasure, and happiness.

It would seem we need to give family life another dimension of meaning and purpose beyond family values—a family need for God, religion, and church—a larger structure for family life.

I feel sure we want to preserve the Catholic heritage for our children—this ancient, rich, beautiful culture of wisdom, intellect, history, art, music, and celebration of life in all its forms and expressions. But if the children are not brought to Mass at an early age, they may never become Catholic.

In a lighter vein, don't we all need, periodically and consistently, to reconnect with our Catholic identity—all that stuff from growing up Catholic we talked about in the first letter—just to give continuity to our lives? And don't we have an existential need for the presence of the Church at major passages in life and death.

The Catholic faith cannot live in a vacuum. It will die. For most Catholics, Mass is where our faith is celebrated and what keeps it alive.

Love,

Dad

48

Letter 14: The Seven Sacraments

Dear Family:

Early on we talked about the Catholic principle of Sacramentality, wherein all of creation is permeated with the presence of God. The Seven Sacraments of the Church fit into this principle in a special way.

And so the old definition goes: "A sacrament is an outward sign instituted by Christ to give grace." The sacraments are physical signs of the presence and grace of the Risen Lord in special rituals of the Church, from the cradle to the grave.

We receive some sacraments, such as baptism and matrimony, at special moments in our lives, but the grace of these sacraments lives on. We receive other sacraments regularly, such as the Eucharist, to deepen the faith and grace within us.

After baptism, the Eucharist is the central event and sacrament of the Catholic Church, where Christ himself is the gift of grace. We have pretty well covered the Eucharist.

The Catechism of the Catholic Church lays out the meaning of Baptism. Baptism is the sacrament of faith. The catechumen or godparents are asked: "What do you want of God's Church?" The response is: "Faith!"

The symbolism of the immersion in water (or pouring of water) is the dying and rising with Christ. The immersion is the death of sin (the Original Sin) and the powers of darkness. The rising out of the water is rising to the new life of grace in Christ and the Holy Spirit. We become truly daughters and sons of God.

Baptism makes us members of the Body of Christ, and initiates us into the Church. We are welcomed at once by the faith community. This is especially dramatic where the local church celebrates baptism during Mass, with big applause afterwards. The godparents assume a responsibility to nurture and educate the new Christian in the Catholic faith.

"Baptism of desire" means that those are considered baptized who are ignorant of the Gospel of Christ and his Church, but seek the truth and do the will of God in accordance with their understanding of it.

Confirmation is also a sacrament, but may be considered as part of the sacrament of baptism. The new Church protocol calls for the administration of confirmation at an early age. The presider prays for the sevenfold gift of the Holy Spirit and, with the laying on of the hand, anoints the forehead of the candidate, saying "Be sealed with the gift of the Holy Spirit." The candidate is thus confirmed and strengthened for the mission of the Church.

In the olden days when we were confirmed around twelve years, it was understood we were now to be "Soldiers of Christ," and the Bishop gave us a little slap upside the head to toughen us up.

Matrimony is a covenant sealed by an "irrevocable personal consent." The true practice of conjugal love, and the whole nature of family life resulting from it, is of equal importance with the begetting of children.

The sacrament of marriage is not something added to the marriage union, rather the mutual exchange of love *is* the sacrament. As Thomas Rausch says: "Marriage is not so much a sacrament a couple receives as a sacrament they become." And to quote Father Nigro: "In the wedding ceremony the couple initiate each other into a life-ling 'marrying' process, and remain life-long sacraments to each other, mediating God's grace into each other in all they are and do, especially in all expressions of love and concern."

On a practical level, it should be remembered that matrimony, as a sacrament, is a powerful source of God's actual grace for those rough patches in married life. Call on that grace.

"Holy Order(s) is a sacrament by which members of the Church are ordained for the ministerial service of the Church as bishops, presbyters [priests] and deacons." The first formal ministry in the Church was that of the Twelve, who were charismatic missionaries. By the end of the first century, the beginning of structure appeared with the commissioning of bishops, priests, and deacons. It was not until the twelfth century that celibacy was made the subject of universal Church legislation, following a monastic model of the priesthood that emerged in the early Middle Ages. Holy Order is commitment to a life dedicated to God, and certainly requires the grace attendant to the sacrament.

See my earlier letter regarding the ordination of women priests and a married clergy.

The sacrament of Reconciliation was formerly known as Confession to you regular sinners. But we don't hear much about sin and Confession any more. Somehow sin has done a makeover so it's hard to recognize. Or else we're all getting holier as we grow older.

Anyhow, if we're in big trouble we know where to go, and we know that it's Jesus in there who is forgiving our sin. There is nothing he would rather do than forgive sin. "People who are in good health do not need a doctor... I have come to call, not the self-righteous, but sinners."

I know some dioceses are now pushing the new Rite of Reconciliation, the public liturgy emphasizing reconciliation with God and each other. I'll still take the box, *mano a mano*. If there's one thing the Church ought to have learned in 2,000 years it is the great spiritual-psychological-emotional relief of individual person-to-person confession.

The Anointing of the Sick (formerly Extreme Unction) is not a sacrament reserved for those at the point of death, but for those who are sick or in some danger of death from injury, sickness or old age (the last sacrament to be administered to the dying is the Viaticum, literally "food for the journey"—the Eucharist). The anointing is not only for the grace of healing, but also for solidarity with Christ in his passion and death as our offering for the world, and especially for our own loved ones.

In conclusion, the sacraments bring to fruition the Catholic belief that Jesus is God Incarnate, and that by visible signs he communicates to us his active, living presence and the grace of God at every Eucharist, and at the major passages and special circumstances of life. We are a sacramental church, heartened and emboldened by the physical presence of God.

Love,

Dad

Letter 15: Last Things

Dear Family:

This letter completes our journey through Catholic theology to the "Last Things": death, judgment, personal resurrection, and eternal happiness with God and each other. I think we need to start with the Communion of Saints.

Catholics believe that all the living and dead, Catholic and non-Catholic, are united in the Holy Spirit in what we call the Communion of Saints. "Saints" (big "S") are those exemplars of heroic virtue particularly honored. But everybody gets to be a saint (small "s") from baptism on. Our communion in the Mystical Body of Christ will be brought to bodily fulfillment in the general resurrection at the end-time.

Our dead are not fading memories, gone forever. They are real. We simply know in our hearts that they are still with us, just over there on the other side. We pray for them, and we pray to them to intercede with God for our needs (I know this isn't very logical— it's the Catholic version of "the fix"—but it seems to work). Sometimes they are patrons or mentors. But mostly we just remember them, feel they are part of our lives, and know that one day we will join them.

Our Catholic belief in the Communion of Saints humanizes the Catholic response to death. Death is part of life, part of our culture, not to be pretended away. In Catholicism, morbid fear and timidity do not surround death. Rather the Catholic response to death is reverent familiarity and compassion: a strong sense of being with each other and the loved one who is gone. While the thought of our own death gives us pause, at some point we come to terms with that, too, and continue on living fully each day as it comes.

And so the question, "Is there really life after death?" doesn't touch us in a serious way because our faith would make no sense at all if we didn't believe we are living a life that is going somewhere.

Because the Catholic imagination is so filled with this idea of the Communion of Saints, most of us probably have the impression that heaven is a warm and friendly place, and it will be a great joy to be united with all our loved ones and friends there, and all those other interesting people. As you know, one of your mother's little idiosyncrasies is to regularly include Shakespeare, Michelangelo and Bach among those she likes to remember in her prayers and looks forward to meeting.

I think this is a good place to mention the Assumption of Mary into heaven. In 1950, backed by most of the bishops of the Church, Pope Pius XII declared that Mary, when her life was complete, was taken up body and soul into heaven.

This teaching carries with it a long tradition in the Catholic Church dating back to the sixth century. No one has pressed an argument against this teaching, probably because of the fundamental belief of the Church in the resurrection of the body, and the feeling that such a gracious act of God was not untimely but entirely fitting in the case of his own mother.

But heaven is more than the human happiness I have tried to describe. It is a divine happiness, the fulfillment of all human desire, in the fullness of life called the Beatific Vision. Richard McBrien writes:

"The Beatific Vision is the full union of the human person with God. It is toward which every person strives... It is the completion of all that we are as human beings."

And as St. Paul tells us:

Eye has not seen, ear has not heard,
nor has it so much as dawned on man,
what God has prepared for those who love him.

For those who would like a little deeper discussion of the meaning of death itself, I have inserted in the notes some material from the philosopher Martin Heidegger and the theologian Karl Rahner.

The Church teaches that at death a person undergoes judgment, called the "particular judgment." Monika Hellwig argues that death itself it the judgment of the individual. Death itself condemns all that embodies selfishness, but it is the consummation of all that embodies love and generosity.

54

Therefore, to the extent we have opened ourselves to love in this life we will each have different capacities for eternal happiness, but we will each find our own happiness complete.

What about Purgatory and Hell? Are they still around? There is a hierarchy of importance in Catholic teaching. If Purgatory, Hell, Angels, Satan, and Demons leave you behind, I wouldn't worry about it. I'm just trying to cover all the bases.

The Catechism of the Catholic Church recognizes Purgatory as a state of repentance, conversion, and purification for those who die in God's friendship, but still need to achieve the holiness necessary to enter the joy of heaven. It is an ancient tradition of the Church, and affirmed by several councils, including Vatican II.

Joseph Dania writes: "At its core, the doctrine affirms simply a transitional spiritual state (possibly instantaneous and coincident with death) of transformation in view of the assured prospect of the Beatific Vision."

At any rate, Catholics still pray for the souls in Purgatory, and especially on All Souls' Day, Nov. 2, the day after All Saints' Day, and November is still the month of the Holy Souls. But most of us don't make that much of a distinction anymore between the "Poor Souls" and the rest of the Communion of Saints. We just pray to and for and with them all.

Then there's Hell, which means a state of total alienation from God. God doesn't punish with fire and brimstone, despite even the metaphorical rhetoric of Jesus. The sinner punishes himself by total alienation from God and his fellow humans through deliberate wickedness. The Catholic Church has never held that anyone is actually in Hell, but holds out the possibility to emphasize that the choices in life are serious.

Even so, it is hard to imagine God condemning someone to such a terrible eternal punishment. While not official Church teaching, the Dutch theologian, Edward Schillebeeckx, suggests a way out of the dilemma. God leaves each of us to our own freedom. The good have chosen solidarity with their fellow human beings and communion with God, and will know a life beyond death because God can receive them. The life of the evil person will simply end. God can only leave evil to its own, limited logic.

On the other hand, Father Nigro suggests it is never too late with God. The lives of human beings are immortal. Death does not end our freedom to choose.

What about angels, Satan, and demons? The Catechism of the Catholic Church treats literally the existence of Satan and his accompanying demons as forces of evil opposed to God and the building of the Kingdom of God, and who can inflict spiritual and physical injury on human beings.

Theologians are divided on the question of Satan. Many modern theologians consider Satan a symbol of evil forces, a personification of evil, rather than a personal spiritual figure.

While the personal existence of Satan has never been defined as an article of faith, both Scripture and tradition have consistently treated Satan as someone real, possessing real power to tempt and to inflict evil, both in individual lives and in the structures of society. Jesus refers to Satan in the most personal terms. Jesus "cast out" demons. Evil spirits are "exorcised" even today. These events can be rationalized simply as interventions in cases of psychological disorder. Yet one wonders.

Angels, on the other hand, are a much happier subject. The Church has no reservations about the existence of angels. They are personal, spiritual, intelligent, immortal beings created by God at the beginning of creation. Jesus often referred to the angels, and we see their presence throughout Scripture. "Angel" means "messenger." Angels are the servants and messengers of God, who live continuously in God's presence, yet the whole Church benefits from their help.

Thus we live in a world surrounded by angelic spirits and other spirits not so benevolent, but all of whom add to the character of Catholic life. Here's a charming little prayer from the Liturgy of the Hours, the Night Prayer your mother and I say on Sunday night:

Lord,
we beg you to visit this house

and banish from it
all the deadly power of the enemy.
May your holy angels dwell here
to keep us in peace
and may your blessing be upon us always.
We ask this through Christ our Lord.

At death the individual experiences the self-revelation or particular judgment (described above by Monika Hellwig) and goes on to union with God (except for any necessary purification in Purgatory, possibly instantaneous), awaiting the resurrection of the body on the last day.

The Church teaches that at the end of time there will be a general resurrection of all the dead through the power of the Holy Spirit. The resurrection of Christ is the promise of this new life.

As with the Risen Lord, this is not a continuation of our former life. Paul tells us we will be transformed in a way appropriate to our new existence (I'll settle for 33). We are immortal spirit-bodies, not just immortal souls. This doesn't mean the reconstitution of a particular matrix of atoms, none of which are the same throughout our mortal life anyhow. It means the resurrection of our whole selves and our continuity as whole persons, as finally complete.

The Second Coming of Christ is simply the final stage of the one coming of Christ, who continues to be with us here at the end, and hands us over to the Father, saved and transformed in him.

At the same time, the Communion of Saints has come to full fruition in bodily form, and we can share the completeness of union with God by our communion with one another.

To end on a lighter note, Monika Hellwig, a practical lady, advised us not to get too hung up on the imagery of how this will all come about. The important thing is that *together* "in our flesh we will see God." We have a community of destiny in this world and in the next.

Thus ends our story of God, creation, salvation, and eternal happiness. God is the Alpha and Omega. I trust you will realize

that beneath all of the wonderful stories, rich traditions, and beautiful rituals of the Catholic faith there is a coherent core of mystical
reality that can appeal both to the intellect and the heart, and to our
hope for a meaningful and purposeful life, here and now and forever.

Love,

  Dad

Letter 16: Self, Virtue, and Morality

Dear Family:

The practice of faith requires a healthy sense of self, the building of character and self-control (virtue), and the living of a responsible life guided by a well-informed conscience (morality).

Concerning self, God has commanded us to love and respect ourselves. Jesus said the second greatest commandment of the law of Moses was to love others *the same as* we love ourselves.

One needs a healthy ego to have a healthy relationship with self, others, and God. We "renounce ourselves" only in the sense that we don't perceive ourselves as the center of the universe, and are therefore unable to be open to God and others because we must constantly maintain our protective mechanisms. "Losing one's life" means finding it in relationship to God and others.

One cannot be of much use to others unless one has a good sense of one's self. Honesty = humility = self-confidence and outgoing love. I think Mother Theresa had a very strong ego, and tremendous self-confidence, and she's a saint.

Now onto the subject of virtue. Christians—Catholics are called to orient our lives towards God ("conversion") with our "whole heart." Conversion is a process of change and growth, not a single dramatic moment in our life. Conversion is a product of virtue, prayer, self-giving service, and the grace of God.

Virtues are habits that enable us to become our authentic self, a person capable of responding fully to God, others, and the demands of life, with the help of God's grace. In short, a person of character.

The four "Cardinal" Virtues (cardinal means "hinge") are Prudence, Justice, Fortitude, and Temperance (taken up by Christianity from Stoic philosophy). They are "human" virtues.

- *Prudence* is the habit of discerning and choosing in each situation our true good and the right way to act upon it.

- *Justice* is giving God and others what is due them, and includes fairness, honesty, and keeping promises.
- *Fortitude* is courage. Courage strengthens us to take bold action, but also to face and endure pain, loss, suffering, and death, and to overcome obstacles to good.
- *Temperance* ("moderation") is the virtue of self-control that enables us to achieve balance in our appetites and passions in order to develop the whole person.

The three "Theological" Virtues are Faith, Hope, and Love. They are called "theological" because they are oriented towards God.
- *Faith* in this context is the virtue of accepting God's self-revelation and entrusting oneself to God. *Faith is basically trust in God.*
- *Hope* is the virtue of trust in the promises of Christ regarding eternal life, and the virtue of working now for the transformation of the world (the Kingdom of God). *Hope is confidence in the future.*
- *Love* is the fulfillment of Christ's commandment, "Love one another as I have loved you." This means loving with self-giving love, in union with Christ's self-giving love. *Love is openness, and responsiveness.*

There are three other virtues that make life a lot easier, and result in enjoying God's gift of peace.
- *Humility* is honest acceptance of our capabilities and limitations, our dependence on God, and what happens in life. Humility is trust and confidence in ourselves as we really are and life as it really is, knowing that God is with us in everything. We change that which needs changing, and accept what we cannot change.
- *Forgiveness* enables us to forgive ourselves and others as we have been forgiven by God and to let go of our faults and the faults of others. Forgiveness is the ultimate freedom to love.

  I would add that, while anger must always be controlled, anger must sometimes be first felt and appropriately ex-

60

pressed in order to work through to the forgiveness of others (including God and the Church). Jesus himself displayed righteous anger on several occasions.

- *Acceptance* (in the sense used here) is the positive regard of others as persons of unique and equal dignity before God, regardless of their station in life or idiosyncrasies. Acceptance rejects judgmentalism. Acceptance requires us to first accept ourselves.

The fruit of all genuine virtue is *peace* and *joy* from the right relationship with God, which results in a right relationship with oneself, each other, and all of creation. It is a condition of wholeness, harmony, and presence of God. We can share this peace and joy with others.

Duly armed with self-understanding and virtue, we can now tackle the otherwise intimidating business of morality.

First: *sin.* Sin is the damaging of our relationships with God, neighbor, and self. Sin is lack of fidelity to God's will. Sin is related to freedom.

Freedom is the essence of being a real person. To be free is to be one's authentic self, to be in possession of one's self, to be responsible for oneself, and to self-determine our choices. Freedom is the capacity to shape our life, and who we are ultimately, in the presence of God. It is the capacity and choice to say "Yes" or "No" to God.

Mortal sin is a rupture of our fundamental relationship with God. It is a fundamental "No" to God with our whole being. I don't think too many of us have to worry about mortal sin, although it was a biggy in the bad old days when some of us were growing up and got petrified of going to Hell because of lack of sensitivity and judgment on the part of well-meaning religious teachers. That has changed, thank God.

Venial sin is an act not consistent with our fundamental orientation toward God, but not a choice against God. Venial sin has degrees of seriousness, depending upon the objective nature of the act, the motives or intention, and the circumstances.

The Catholic Church has historically grounded its moral teaching on "natural law," in addition to the revelation of God in the Old Testament (the Ten Commandments) and the Gospel of Christ. Natural law is derived from the reflection of human reason on human nature and human experience. It is said we discover the natural law in the depths of our heart. The traditional moral teaching of the Church is based upon duty and law, rights and privileges, and is primarily *objective*, holding that some actions are inherently wrong no matter what the purpose or circumstances.

However, since Vatican II, many Catholic theologians and philosophers (sometimes known as "revisionists") have questioned the inflexibility of the natural law approach. They view the Christian moral life primarily in terms of the Christian's multiple relations with God, neighbor, world, and self. This might be called the *relational* model of moral theology, although it does not exclude objective norms.

The revisionist theologians propose a theory called *proportionalism*. While rejecting utilitarianism (the end justifies the means), this approach weighs the intent, circumstances, and foreseeable consequences, and the proportion between the values and disvalues, of actions. The action becomes morally wrong when, all things considered, there is no proportionate reason to justify an exception to objective behavioral norms. It should be said that the magisterium of the Church rejects propotionalism.

Conscience is our personal guide to appropriate moral behavior. Conscience is not a *feeling* of what's right or wrong based on a feeling of guilt or lack of guilt, but rather a *judgment* whether something is good or bad. Our pure "gut feeling" or unformed opinion may be wrong. We are obliged to inform our conscience in good faith, if necessary by consulting with other people or sources, and the teaching of the Church.

But in the end we must act in accordance with our convictions and be true to ourselves, right or wrong. We are judged finally by God on the basis of what is in our hearts, i.e. our honest convictions, not what we do. One classic sign of a good decision is peace of mind. We have no more real questions about the matter.

62

Vatican II taught: *"To obey [one's conscience] is the very dignity of the human person; according to it the person will be judged. Conscience is the most secret core and sanctuary of a person. There the person is alone with God, whose voice echoes in the depths of the person."*

The exercise of conscience is guided by the cardinal virtue of *prudence*. What is the right thing for me to do in this situation in the light of my relationships and responsibilities? The exercise of conscience may require prayerful reflection and discernment under the guidance of the Spirit.

Love,

Dad

All you who are thirsty,
come to the water!
You who have no money,
come, receive grain and eat;
Come, without paying and without cost,
drink wine and milk!
Why spend your money for what is not bread;
your wages for what fails to satisfy?

For my thoughts are not your thoughts,
nor are your ways my ways, says the Lord.
As high as the heavens are above the earth,
so high are my ways above your ways
and my thoughts above your thoughts.

-Isaiah

Letter 17: Catholic Spirituality

Dear Family:

"Practice the Presence of God," said St. Thomas Aquinas, when he'd had enough of theology. *"Wake up!"* said the Jesuit mystic, Anthony de Mello—God is *here*, not *there*, within, all around, like the air we breathe. Spirituality is the habit of being aware of and responding to God's presence.

Prayer is the heart of all spirituality. Prayer satisfies our built-in human desire for a deep, direct, personal relationship with God, and the integration of our true selves. "O Lord, you have made us for yourself, and our heart is restless until it rests in you." (Augustine).

Prayer is the opening of our mind and heart to the presence of God. It is the act by which we enter into conscious communion with God. Prayer is whatever we want it to be, and has no set words, no set time, no set place. Yet, except for spontaneous prayers during the day, it may be best to set aside five or ten minutes at the same time and the same place each day for a quiet time with God. Perhaps simply setting aside that time with God is more important than the content—just showing up, letting it happen, being real with God.

At first our prayer may be mostly asking for God's help. As Anne Lamott says in her "Traveling Mercies," her two main prayers are "Help me, help me, help me," and "Thank you, thank you, thank you."

The "thank you" part is particularly important. Gratefulness puts our life in perspective, and opens our heart to God.

We can go from there with prayers for forgiveness of ourselves and others, for strength and courage in our troubles, for guidance with things we have to either accept or change, or for the needs of our family and friends. The Our Father is an apt introduction to such prayers.

Sooner or later we end up talking to God about our life, and sort of "listening" to God's response. From there we can gradually enter into a quiet communion, just being open to the loving presence of God.

One of the dear sisters we know thinks of prayer as just sitting quietly. God is already within us. Just tune in. It's as natural as breathing out and breathing in.

In addition to the "open" approach to prayer I have described above, there are various methodologies.

Whispering or speaking a mantra can help us to actualize God's presence. For example, we can start by being conscious of our breathing, and whisper a simple word as a mantra. We can use any word—God, Abba, Father, Spirit, Jesus, Lord, thank you Lord, yes Lord, love, peace, silence, open, presence, trust, etc. The word and breathing lead us to the presence of God.

Centering Prayer is a passive version of this, something like the prayer methods of the Far East. But in Christianity it is the centering of ourselves with the intention of being open to the presence and action of God within us, without specific goals of thought or feeling. The idea is to let thought flow freely until we become silent in God's presence. A mantra is repeated only as long as is necessary to free the mind of discursive thoughts.

Lectio Divina is a simple way to prayerfully reflect on a short passage of scripture, as if the Lord were speaking directly to us in that passage. The Rosary is a familiar way to reflect on the mysteries of the rosary, or as a mantra to pray for ourselves, family and friends, or to pray in union with the Communion of Saints. (Catholics at times say just Hail Mary, asking for Mary's prayers for a special need or intention, particularly for others.)

Finally, the Liturgy of the Hours is the official vocal prayer of the Church, sung in monasteries continuously night and day throughout the world. Composed of psalms and short prayers, it is recited antiphonally, and is especially useful for married couples, particularly the short night prayer before retiring. It is available in an abbreviated version called "Shorter Christian Prayer."

Any kind of prayer can, sooner or later, lead to contemplation. Contemplation is simply the prayer of quiet. "Be still and know I am God." It is resting in God—beyond thoughts, words, and emotions—resting in the God within who is closer than breathing, closer than consciousness.

We're all curious about *mysticism*. A good definition is "The graced transformation of consciousness that follows on a *direct* or *immediate* experience of the presence of God, leading to deeper union with God." Directness and immediacy is the key. Mysticism is not an elitist concept, requiring visions etc. It may be one of those peak moments in the life of grace that can happen to anyone.

In prayer we come to know our true self because we are in the presence of God. "O Lord, you have probed me and you know me; you know when I sit and when I stand. Truly you have formed my inmost being; you knit me in my mother's womb." (Psalm 139)

Henri Nouwen says we must come to know and believe we are the "beloved" of God, that the real trap in life is not arrogance but self-rejection. The core truth of our existence is God's voice saying within us: "You are my beloved, on you my favor rests."

While speaking of prayer, we shouldn't overlook children's prayer. In my experience kids like grace before meals, and especially a prayer together before going to bed, along with a song or two. Make it a custom. Kids like customs.

We have talked about practicing the presence of God in prayer. That is the foundation of spirituality. But spirituality is broader

66

than prayer. Spirituality is practicing the presence of God in all creation and in everyday life. It includes both living in God's grace within us, and in seeing God's presence in everything surrounding us.

Grace (L. gratis—gift) is the completion of God's tremendous gift of life—the gift of God's own personal life and self *within us*. The *Catechism* calls this "participation" in the life of God.

The theologian Roger Haight says this participation is not static, but rather means new capacity, energy, and empowerment in cooperation with God's Spirit.

We can experience this grace as God's love. God is love, and God's grace is love. We can learn to live in God's love by loving ourselves, by being open to the love of others, by giving to others the love God gives to us, by being grateful to God for all of God's gifts, and by prayer.

Roger Haight makes this telling statement about God's love:

"The liberating effect of grace lies precisely in God's acceptance of human beings as they are. Grace means that God is the lover of every single human being, infinitely and as if there were not other, with a love that makes each person infinitely valuable despite sin."

Grace is called "eternal life" in the Gospel of John, and in Catholic liturgy, meaning life in God both now and hereafter. As we have seen, we have received this gift through the death and resurrection of Christ, which is re-presented at every Mass, and by our baptism.

The habitual indwelling of God is what the Church calls habitual grace or sanctifying grace. The grace we need and call upon for help and guidance in life situations is called actual grace- the intervening power of God. Actual graces are promptings by God to help us to know what to do and to give us the strength to do it.

We call upon God to help us to sort ourselves out, to help us get through a tough day, to give us strength and courage and confidence when we need it, to help us do the right thing in various situations, to help us succeed with our project, to give us inspiration, to help us trust life and be positive, to help us forgive and accept ourselves and others and our entire life, to help us to love and to be loved.

But although the Church still makes the distinction between habitual grace and actual grace, modern theology holds that there's a seamless relationship between habitual grace and actual grace, that it's one and the same grace taken from diverse angles.

What we've been talking about might be thought of as the grace within. What about the outward grace of our personal relationships?

What better place to start than St. Paul's letter to the Corinthians?

"Love is patient, love is kind. Love is not jealous, it does not put on airs, it is not snobbish. Love is never rude, it is not self-seeking, it is not prone to anger; neither does it brood over injuries. Love does not rejoice in what is wrong, but rejoices with the truth. There is no limit to love's forbearance, to its trust, its hope, its power to endure... There are in the end three things that last: faith, hope, and love, and the greatest of these is love."

Here I'll invite your mother to speak of nature and grace:

"All of these things Pail says call for grace, for God's love which transcends our natural love but acts together with our love. Think of grace in terms of love—that's what God's life is. But we have to activate God's life within us—make an effort—make it a habit. We can't just act viscerally in relationships. Grace helps us to respond to others in love rather than anger or getting even. I think kindness and courtesy are grace in action."

Sometimes we recognize people who are grace-filled. Sometimes we have a grace-filled encounter with such a person, if only for a moment. Sooner or later we become sensitized to grace.

Finally, as we discussed in the early letter on Sacramentality, Catholic spirituality "sees" God in all things, the presence of God permeating all of creation, the invisible God made visible, not only in religious symbols, but also in persons, events, objects, nature, the cosmos. Sometimes this sacramental view makes it easier to

68

see the presence of God in our surroundings rather than within ourselves, because our surroundings are visible. God in a flower.

And we are in the presence of God when we are attending to the present moment instead of thinking about ourselves, or wondering what we are going to do next, or tomorrow. The advice of the Desert Fathers of the fourth century to those seeking their true selves and God was, "Do what you're doing." And we recall the Lord said, "Enough, then, of worrying about tomorrow. Let tomorrow take care of itself. Today has troubles enough of its own." Life is what is happening while we are planning something else.

Prayer and grace can lead us to a particular relationship with Christ. The Church speaks of this intimate relationship as living "in Christ." At the Last Supper, Jesus used this simile to tell us just how close this relationship can be:

> *I am the vine, you are the branches.*
> *He who lives in me and I in him*
> *will produce abundantly,*
> *for apart from me you can do nothing.*
> *It was not you who chose me,*
> *it was I who chose you,*
> *to go forth and bear fruit.*
> *Your fruit must endure.*

The idea of living "in Christ" suggests that we are on a path toward becoming more Christ-like, which is the end goal of the Christian life in this world. This process is often referred to as transformation, and is not the work of a day, but the work of a lifetime, although some seem to get there ahead of the rest of us. We can sum up transformation in Christ's words, "He who loses his life for my sake shall find it."

Transformation is not some pious pose, but rather simply becoming the kind of person we really want to be. It is a positive change toward growth and development of our spiritual self—a change from self-absorption to self-abandonment, from a primarily worldly self-image and vision of life to a habitual vision of the presence and love of God within us and surrounding us.

Nor does this mean losing our ego (self-identity), but rather allowing us to "find ourselves" in union with Christ, and in the greater emotional security and peace we develop in knowing our own worth in God's eyes.

=

The Trinity is three Persons in one God, so that the three are always present together. Nevertheless we are able to appropriate to each, separately, certain attributes that are peculiar to that Person, as we do with the Father, and as we have done with life "in Christ." What about the Holy Spirit?

I have occasionally in this letter and elsewhere made reference to the Holy Spirit, but I have not dwelt on a relationship with the Holy Spirit. To quote Barbara Finan: "There is a kind of self-effacing quality to the Spirit's being within and among persons."

Father Yves M.J. Congar puts it this way: "...it has been suggested that the Holy Spirit empties himself, in a kind of kenosis, of his own personality in order to be in a relationship, on the one hand, with "God" and Christ, and, on the other, with [us]...but through what he brings about in us."

The Holy Spirit is God's presence and power in action. God relates to us and to the world through the Holy Spirit and guides us in the Spirit. The Spirit is the "Lord and giver of life," as we say in the Creed. The Spirit is the spirit of unity within us and among us, making of the many a communion with God and each other.

Jesus told us to ask for the gift of the Holy Spirit. It can be liberating to let go, be open to the Spirit, and let the Spirit work in us, pray in us, "breath" in us. As Jesus said, "The wind blows where it will."

Let's wrap up this discussion of spirituality with a brief look at happiness and joy. These attributes have their natural meanings and causes, but have a special meaning in the world of spirituality.

Ask any of us what we really want out of life and we'll say we want to be happy, and we want our loved ones to be happy. Happiness in this life is a matter of good fortune, good habits (virtue), and a good attitude. I strongly recommend the book, *The Saints'*

Guide to Happiness, by Robert Ellsberg, as a lucid and insightful guide to happiness in everyday life.

But the Church defines happiness in terms of eternity, the complete fulfillment of all desires. Happiness is being united with God, the ultimate goal of human existence. Happiness is participation in God's own beatitude or happiness.

What about joy?

On a purely natural level we might equate joy with delight, a pleasurable emotion. But Christian joy goes much deeper.

Jesus said:

> *As the Father has loved me,*
> *so I have loved you.*
> *Live on in my love...*
> *All this I tell you*
> *that my joy may be yours*
> *and your joy may be complete.*

Joy has to do with faith and self-giving love. The Dictionary of the Bible defines joy as "quiet confidence in God." Joy is a gift from God, an actual grace that comes from my belief in God's total love and affirmation of me, in all circumstances (God's will). Come what may we know that "all will be well... and all manner of things will be well" (Julian of Norwich) because that is God's will for me. Or to quote from Jeremiah: "The Lord says: my plans for you are peace and not disaster..."

We know from the experience of our own lives and the lives of others that this deep-down sense of assurance can endure both in good times and bad times, even in the face of suffering and death. Timeless Catholic tradition recognizes a spiritual good in "offering up" our suffering or loss for the good of others, in solidarity with the suffering of Christ and the suffering of the world. With confidence in God's love, we embrace the cross and go for the joy.

Joy is the fruit of living in God's love, the fruit of grace.

Love,
Dad

Letter 18: Catholic Lifestyle

Dear Family:

I could call this letter The Practice of the Faith, since it brings down to action the Catholic teachings we've been talking about. But I prefer "Catholic Lifestyle" because the practice of faith really touches all aspects of life, to a greater or lesser degree, depending on how far you buy into it.

It's simplest to speak in terms of married couples with kids, but most of this applies to singles as well.

But first let's review a few of the basics of the Catholic faith. We hear a lot these days about "family values," and that's all to the good. I'd like to add to family values "Catholic values," those basics of the Catholic faith that we may rather unconsciously carry with us as we live the faith.

We have a Catholic identity, which grounds us in an ancient heritage. We are part of a Catholic community. We have a rich, coherent set of beliefs and traditions that tell us who we are, why we're here, where we're going, and what God expects.

We are "of the earth." We see the material world and earthly beauty and pleasures as good because permeated by the presence of God.

We have habits of prayer that can lead us into the presence of God, help us to call upon God's grace, and help us to live in God's love and bear fruit that will last.

Our central act of worship, the Mass, is a sacrament, a physical sign of the presence of the Risen Lord in our community, and within each of us.

We know that self-giving service to others in need is the hallmark of all Christianity.

We are prepared to embrace both the opportunities and the difficulties and sufferings of life with trust, courage, and self-confidence—and to go for the joy.

With these Catholic values somewhere in the background, we can approach the practice of the faith.

We start with Mass, the sacrament of Jesus' death and resurrection and our new life in the Spirit, which he shares with us at Communion and at every moment of our life. We go forth to share this life with others.

In this world Jesus taught, fed, healed, served, befriended, dined, and laughed. Now it's our turn to imitate him. Sooner or later we begin to realize that *we* mediate his life *bodily* through human relationships. *We* become his voice to witness his Good News in our own unique way.

The energy for this lifestyle is prayer: the 5 or 10 minutes of quiet prayer in the morning, the prayers at meals, the evening prayer. And spontaneously during the day, a quick prayer of our own making, just to stay in touch.

This practice of faith can be conscious or unconscious. If conscious, with St. Paul we intentionally "put on the mind of Christ" in situations where someone has a need and we respond to that need.

But we can also make a difference quite unconsciously by simply being who we are, where we are, doing what we're doing, with those we are near—in the light of our Catholic values.

Abbot Keating tells us:

"People know that somehow Christ is acting in you, is present in you, and is loving them in you. This is the atmosphere in which people can grow and become fully alive. And the greatest love, of course, is divine love, especially when it becomes transparent in another person. *And it is most impressive when that person is not even aware of it and it just happens.*" (emphasis supplied).

But when it comes to *doing*, if self-giving service is the heart of Christianity and Catholicism, you're doing it every day. I'm talking about the activities of your everyday life, from getting the kids dressed in the morning, to working all day in or outside the home, to cooking dinner, to helping each other, to talking on the phone in the evening with a friend or relative who has a problem, to mentoring a talented high school kid from the wrong side of town. Whether we realize it or not, we live and breathe service to someone all day long.

I emphasize this quite deliberately because one can pick up the idea at church that unless one is involved in a church ministry, or reaching out to the poor, one is not engaged in Christian service.

Charity begins at home. Later on you will have the time and the duty to reach out and fill those other needs.

You are also practicing the faith when you practice those everyday habits of thoughtfulness, kindness, and courtesy; openness and responsiveness to the needs of others, taking time to listen; treating everyone as having equal dignity with you; just being cheerful; just being a friend.

And so it seems that wherever we are and whatever we do there's an opportunity to live in God's love and bear fruit that will last.

Does that include our work in the world? How can we make our work meaningful in terms of faith?

The first thing is, *we don't compartmentalize our lives.* We don't wear one hat at Mass, another at home, and another hat at work. It's all the same hat. One hat—one life. It's *all* sacred—sacramental—the presence of God in ordinary material things, in ordinary activities and events, and especially in ordinary people.

Catholicism is in the world and of the world, equally at home with history and philosophy and teaching, science and technology, art and literature and movies, politics and marketing and business, construction, and law and medicine.

It follows that the practice of faith at work is the "spirituality of the ordinary," to use Joseph Allegretti's phrase, in doing what we do each day. Relationships are also as crucial to the workplace as they are anywhere else, as are those habits we talked about earlier such as thoughtfulness, kindness, courtesy, and the rest. Work is its own community. And if you're working downtown you can occasionally pop in for a noon Mass. It gives a whole new dimension to the workweek.

Work is also a place for self-expression and creativity, for adding value to life. Teilhard de Chardin says it best in his own compelling way: "We may, perhaps, imagine that creation was finished long ago. But that would be quite wrong. We serve to complete it, even by the humblest work of our hands. That is, ultimately the meaning and values of our acts... The will to succeed, a certain passionate delight in the work to be done, form an integral part of our creaturely fidelity..."

Above all, work is service. Whatever we do is a service to someone, somewhere, directly or indirectly. "Mankind is our business." And at the end of the day, it is bringing home the paycheck to support our family.

The poet Kahlil Gibran summed up work in his beautiful way: "Work is love made visible."

Work is the way we spend most of our time, but we can't allow work to become an idol. Ambition is good. Competitiveness is good. Money is good, and necessary. Even power can be good if used wisely. But we can't permit our identity, our free time, and our family life to become totally dominated by work. We simply can't do it all perfectly. Here is an opportunity for humility and self-discipline. Each married couple will need to make their own definition of success, the good life and family life, set their priorities, find their balance, and do it their way.

Not forgetting to set aside time for themselves. The sacrament of marriage is ongoing and is fundamentally not about children but about respect, kindness, and self-giving between spouses, about "making one person happy," about fun, romance, and sex. And, if possible, about a certain religious bonding even if the couple is not of the same faith, such as occasionally attending church together, or reading scripture together.

Helpful thought: You don't have to break the bank to go out to dinner together. Your mother and I use to have a little candlelight dinner once a week upstairs in our room while the kids had their dinner downstairs. Everybody was glad to get rid of each other.

The idea of balance. Our Jewish friends learned a long time ago that they needed a day off *every week*. Are Jews compulsive, competitive, hard workers, and generally ahead of the rest of us? So how do they manage this? Go figure. (Helpful hunt: Start with little spaces of time. It'll grow on you, but it takes courage not to work.)

I can't let go of this without mentioning some of those little traditions that allow the practice of the Catholic faith to be human:

Like blessing ourselves with the sign of the cross (three times
by your mother when she's in serious trouble): the "God bless"
whenever we say goodbye; the bringing home of the palm leaf on
Palm Sunday and sticking it behind one of the many crucifixes in
the home; blessing ourselves when we go out; the statues of Mary
and St. Francis in the garden; the holy medal around our necks;
saying a Hail Mary when we hear somebody's got trouble; carrying
a wooden rosary around in our pockets to give away; the prayer to
St. Anthony to find the thing we've lost (never fails); the St.
Christopher medal in the car to protect us from wrecks; lighting
votive candles in church for somebody; the wake the night before
someone's funeral with all the wonderful stories and lies about our
dear departed friend; the Rosary; the Communion of Saints, with
all our loved ones just over there on the other side.

These things weave the faith into the fabric of our everyday
lives in a tangible way, and give us comfort.

Love,

Dad

Letter 19: Summing Up: The Catholic Worldview

Dear Family:

The Catholic worldview is to live in Christ through prayer, the Eucharist, and self-giving service. To live in Christ is to live in grace. Grace is the life of God within us.

God's life is love—God is by nature totally self-giving. God created humankind to share this life of love out of sheer benevolence. But the created human was not capable of receiving this life of God, this grace, without God's help. So God became one of us in Jesus Christ, and by his death and resurrection transformed us into this new life of grace.

The Church—the Catholic community—mediates to us the grace of Christ through Word and Sacrament, primarily in the Mass, but also through each other. The offering of the Eucharist—the Body and Blood of Christ—in thanksgiving, and the sharing of Communion among us, is the center of Catholic life.

Our Catholic faith is kept alive by Mass and prayer. We are spiritual beings and must have spiritual nourishment. Without these sources of spirituality our minds and hearts can become dull and mundane. With them, we can experience real hope and joy.

Jesus preached the Kingdom of God, and the Church continues to hold up the Kingdom of God as the ideal for the life of the world. The Kingdom of God is like a metaphor for the transforming presence and power of God in ourselves, our lives, and our society—here, now, in the future, and at the end of time. Belief in God's ultimate victory over the evils of the world gives us an optimistic view of life.

At the end of time our transformation will be completed by our own bodily resurrection. "In our flesh we shall see God." We will enjoy total happiness in the presence of God and our loved ones and companions in the Communion of Saints. Even in this life we can know the joy of solidarity with all our loved ones and companions, living and dead.

The Catholic faith is sacramental. The Catholic vision "sees" God in all things, the presence of God permeating all of creation, the invisible made visible. God communicates God's presence to us through the material, not only in religious symbols, but also in persons, events, nature, objects, the cosmos. God is present, and the material world and its joys and pleasures are therefore good, even if flawed.

The Catholic faith is a thinking person's faith, Some of the finest minds of 2,000 years have participated in the development and reinterpretation of a coherent theology of the truths of faith. I say "reinterpretation" because as in all things human mistakes have been made along the way and have been amended. There may also be present teachings which may, in God's time, be reformulated because of this persistent search for truth and coherence.

The Catholic lifestyle may be summed up in Christ's commandment, "Love one another as I have loved you." We can make a difference by simply being who we are, where we are, doing what we're doing, with those we are near—in the light of Christ's commandment and our Catholic values.

Love,

Dad

Attend, my people, to my teaching;
listen to the words of my mouth.
I will open my mouth in story,
drawing lessons from of old.
We have heard them, we know them;
our ancestors have recited them to us.
We do not keep them from our children;
we recite them to the next generation,
the praiseworthy and mighty deeds of the Lord,
the wonders that he performed.
God set up a decree in Jacob,
established a law in Israel:
What he commanded our ancestors,
they were to teach their children;
that the next generation might come to know,
children yet to be born.
In turn they were to recite them to their children,
that they too might put their trust in God.

- Psalm 78

Epilogue: Some Practical Advice

Dear Family:

In these letters I've tried to distill my own belief in the Catholic faith – after a lot of research and consultation with others. These letters are really for myself as well as for you, for my grandchildren, and for your contemporaries of this generation.

I hope that you, too, will take the Catholic faith seriously, give this little book a close reading, argue with it, agree where you can, and over time come up with your own interpretation of the Catholic faith that you can live with. Only then can you begin to make mature, responsible, and well- considered judgments about the role the Catholic faith will play in your life and the lives of your children.

I hope this apologetic of the Catholic faith will help you to better understand the faith at a more intellectual level than when you first learned it as a child. As I said in the introduction, you need to be thinking Catholics, and know what the Church really stands for. But to be a thinking Catholic you need to have the wisdom to accept truths that are in the spiritual dimension, and not be bound by materialistic, mechanistic logic. You need to allow for mystery in order to know and enjoy the fullness of life. "Critical thinking" can take you only so far.

What if you still have difficulty with belief? Everyone has difficulty with belief at some point in their life. I lost my faith when I was in college, after my brother's death. But I hung on and came back.

I hope you will take the risk to be religious, and get on with life. Humankind has never gotten far without religion if life is to have meaning and purpose. That's what religion is all about.

If you possibly can, be Catholic, in your own way. I'm good at lighting candles. I'll light one for you. The main thing is to take it easy and light, attend Mass whenever you can, and do some family prayer in the home. Sooner or later God will show you the way forward. For now, just show up.

Thanks for your patience in reading this book. Keep the faith.

Love and God Bless,

Dad

NOTES

The Modern Catholic Encyclopedia (Collegeville: The Liturgical Press, 1994) is abbreviated as *Encyc/Liturgical.*

The HarperCollins Encyclopedia of Catholicism (San Francisco: HarperSanfrancisco, 1995) is abbreviated as *Encyc/Harper.*

I should state at the outset that I have not found it necessary for my purposes to cite chapter and verse of the various quotations from scripture I've used throughout the book. For the most part they are taken from The New American Bible (New York: Catholic Publishers, Inc., 1971), an old standby.

Letter 2: Catholic Community and Universality

I have drawn upon Richard P. McBrien's discussion of the mediation of the community in his *Catholicism* (San Francisco: HarperSanfrancisco, 1994), at p. 1197.

Letter 3: Catholic Sacramentality

I have adapted Father McBrien's exposition of the Catholic principle of sacramentality found at p. 10 of *Catholicism,* and thereafter throughout the book.

The quotation from Father Andrew Greeley is taken from his book, *The Catholic Myth* (New York: Touchstone, 1990).

The quotation from Monica Hellwig is found at p. 776 of *Encyc/Liturgical.*

Letter 4 : Catholic Rationality

See extended discussion of theology in McBrien, *Catholicism,* pp. 40 et. seq.

Letter 5: The Sources of Catholic Teaching

The beginning material here is based upon Avery Dulles' article, Faith and Revelation, in Volume II of *Systematic Theology* (Minneapolis: Fortress Press, 1991). The quotation regarding events in history is found at p. 95.

I consulted the Dulles article on the interpretation of scripture, but the breakdown of the historical-critical method is taken from Raymond Collins' article, Interpretation of Scripture, *Encyc/Harper*, beginning at p. 1173, with help from my scripture-scholar wife, Elizabeth. The historical-critical method includes:

(1) *Text criticism,* seeking to establish the original text; (2) *exegesis,* seeking the meaning intended by the author; (3) *source criticism* – what were the potentially oldest written witnesses to the events? (4) *historical criticism*—what was going on in the world of the subject (e.g. the political and religious climate of Palestine at the time of Jesus), and why or for whom the document was written (did Mark write his Gospel for the suffering Gentile Christian community in Rome?).

Then on to (5) *form criticism,* which studies the various generic literary forms in use in the Bible; (6) *literary criticism,* which takes up the fascinating questions of literary genre (the story of Adam and Eve is in the form of a myth, but what truth does the myth convey? (7) and finally, *redaction criticism*—how did the biblical authors work creatively with the available documentary material and oral tradition to weave together these stories we now know as the Bible?

On the subject of tradition I consulted Dulles and McBrien.

The quote regarding the *sensus fidelium* is from the article of that title by Roger Haight in *Encyc/Harper*, p.1182. The Vatican II reference to the *sensus fidelium* is from the *Dogmatic Constitution on the Church*, n. 12.

The quotation from the encyclopedia is from Peter C. Phan's article on the Magisterium at p. 537.

Letter 6: What Does the Church Teach?

On the nature and holiness of God I consulted generally Catherine Mowry LaCugna's article, The Trinitarian Mystery of God, in *Systematic Theology,* Vol.I, p.149; Michael Downey's article on Holiness in *Encycl/Liturgical* p.384; Rudolph Otto, *The Idea of the Holy* (London: Oxford University Press, 1958); and the *Catechism of the Catholic Church* (Rome: Libreria Editrice Vaticana, 1994), beginning at paragraph 214.

The description of the nature and relationships of the Father, Son, and Spirit is adapted from McBrien's theological synthesis of the Triune God, beginning at p.321, with additional reference to the *Catechism,* beginning at paragraph 249. The quotation from the *Catechism* is at paragraph 221.

The quotation from Elizabeth Johnson is from her article, Creation, in *Encyc/Harper.*

On human beings giving glory to God, see Humbert Bouesse's article on the Glory of God in the *Sacramentum Mundi* (New York: The Seabury Press, 1975).

Those interested in the evolutionary aspect of the ongoing process of creation can tackle Karl Rahner's article on Evolution in the *Sacramentum Mundi.* Also of interest are Denis Edwards' *Jesus and the Cosmos* (New York, Paulist Press, 1991), and the works of Pierre Teilhard de Chardin. *God After Darwin* by John F. Haught is published by Westview Press, Boulder, 2000. Father Haught is rector of the Georgetown University Center for the Study of Science and Religion.

For a general discussion of sin and grace, see McBrien, Catholicism, Chapter V, and the article Sin and Grace, by Roger Haight, in *Systematic Theology*, Vol. II, p. 75.

On Original Sin, see McBrien pp. 184 et.seq.; Haight, Sin and Grace; Rahner, *Foundations of Christian Faith* (New York: Crossroad,1995, *pp.*106 et.seq.); Smith (*Encyc/Harper,pp.*943 et.seq.) ; Fagan (*Encyc/Liturgical,* pp. 620 et.seq). On personal sin, see McBrien at 1251 (Glossary).

Support for the proposition that sin (except mortal sin) does not mean the loss of God's grace is found in Richard A. McCormick's article on Sin in *Encyc/Harper*; and in Sean Fagan's article on Sin in *Encyc/Collegeville*. I discuss the effects of mortal sin in a later letter.

The definition of "salvation" is adapted from McBrien's Glossary at p.1250.

The quotation, "From the beginning…" is from the *Catechism* at paragraph 280. See, further, Rahner, *Foundations of Christian Faith*, pp.282-284; and McBrien, pp. 494-499.

The quotation, "the whole of the creative process…" is from McBrien, p.257.

See also the excellent article by Kenneth R. Overberg, S.J., *The Incarnation, God's Gift of Love* found in the publication *Scripture From Scratch*, December 2001 (Cincinnati: St. Anthony Messenger Press, 2001). Father Overberg shows how understanding the incarnation as part of God's original plan of creative love can dramatically change our image of God from a vindictive God—demanding the suffering and death of Jesus as a payment for past sin—to a gracious God, sharing divine life and love in creation and in the incarnation, like parents sharing their love in the life of a new child.

Letter 8: The Church and Sex

Roe v. Wade may be found at 410 U S 113, 35 L Ed 2d 147, 93 S Ct 705 (1973).

See, generally, Carol A. Tauer's article on Abortion in *Encyc/Harper*, and particularly at p.7 regarding the gestational age of the full human being. There is, in fact, a difference of opinion between Catholic theologians, consulting with biologists, whether the embryo is a full human being at fertilization or after 14 days, but for the purposes of this letter that is not really relevant. In any event, most theologians go with the metaphysical analysis that human life begins at fertilization.

The reference to gestational age at the time the heart begins to beat is found in *Color Atlas of Clinical Embryology*, p. 11, (Philadelphia: W. B. Saunders Company, 1994).

Letter 10: The Life of Jesus

I mentioned that I would provide some ancient collateral references to the existence of Jesus. I draw from a brief account by Gerald O'Collins at p. 2 of his *Christology* (New York: Oxford University Press, 1995.)

"Such non-Christian sources as the Roman writers Tacitus, Suetonius, and Pliny the Younger, the Jewish historian Flavius Josephus (whose testimony suffers from later interpolations), and, later, the Cynic philosopher Lucian of Samosata and the Babylonian Talmud yield a little data about Jesus: he was put to death by crucifixion under the Roman prefect Pontius Pilate during the reign of the Emperor Tiberius; some Jewish leaders in Jerusalem were involved in the execution; his followers called him "Christ" and regarded him as the divine founder of a new way of life."

The discussion of the virgin birth is based on McBrien, *Catholicism, pp.539-545.*

The material on "Jesus the Natzorean," and the possible marriage arrangement between Mary and Joseph, is taken from Pixner, *With Jesus Through Galilee According to the Fifth Gospel* (Israel: Corazin Publishing; Collegeville: The Liturgical Press, 1992).

The story, chronology, and approximate dates of Jesus' ministry in Galilee are taken from Pixner. Father Pixner (d.2002, R.I.P.) was a Benedictine Monk, scripture scholar, and archaeologist who lived at the monastery at Tabgha on the Sea of Galilee for nearly twenty years, and had become thoroughly familiar with the topography, distances, and seasons of Galilee. After making all the necessary disclaimers regarding speculation, Father Pixner prepared this beautiful book replete with photographs, maps, and time charts which attempts to reconstruct the chronology of Jesus' ministry in Galilee, relying primarily on the Gospel of Mark.

Father Pixner makes a convincing argument at pp. 69-70 of his book that there were two feedings of the multitude (contra John). Likewise at pp. 97-98 he makes a convincing argument that the "high mountain" of the Transfiguration was Mt. Hermon and not Mt. Tabor.

See McBrien, *Catholicism,* pp. 339-342 for the material and quote on miracles.

Letter 11: The Jesus of Faith

In general, see the *Catechism*, p. 338.

On the new covenant as a covenant of love with God and one another, see O'Collins' article on Redemption in *Encyc/Harper*, p. 1090.

The reference to Anselm and the tradition of Christ's "satisfaction" for our sins is found in O'Collins' article on Atonement at p. 110 op. cited.

On Christ's passion and death, see O'Collins, *Christology,*p. 287 regarding Jesus' "dealing with sin."

For Rahner on death as a definitive act, see his article on Death in *Sacramentum Mundi*, p.329 et. seq. At p. 332 Rahner articulates the meaning of Christ's sacrificial death as reconciliation with God in this fashion: "It is precisely by its darkness that the death of Christ becomes the expression and embodiment of his loving obedience, *the free transference of his entire created existence to God.*" What more could Jesus as representative of humanity give to the Father to achieve "At-one-ment" (atonement) for our sins?

On Christ's resurrection as "metahistorical," the quotation from McBrien is found at p. 435 of *Catholicism*.

On Christ's death and resurrection as being one saving event, see Rahner, *Sacramentum Mundi*, p. 332, and *Foundations of Faith*, p.266.

Letter 12: The Jesus of the Eucharist

Anthony D. Andreassi ascribes the earliest fully-formed Eucharistic prayer to Hippolytus of Rome (ca. 215). See his article, Eucharistic Prayer, *Encyc/Liturgical*, p. 296.

Joseph Quinn mentions that the Gloria was used in the morning prayers as far back as the fourth century. See his article on Gloria in Excelsis Deo, *Encyc/Liturgical*, p. 346.

See David N. Powers' article on the Eucharist, *Systematic Theology*, Vol. II, p.283, regarding the transformation of our own human lives and hopes in the offering of the Eucharist.

The quotation from Richard McBrien on the Eucharist as table fellowship and sacred banquet is found at p. 830 of *Catholicism.*

Letter 14: The Seven Sacraments

On Baptism, see paragraphs 1213-1274 of the *Catechism.*

On Confirmation, see McBrien, *Catholicism,* pp. 818-819.

Regarding Matrimony, the quote from Rausch is at p.101 of his *Catholicism.*

The quote from McBrien on Holy Order is at p. 1241 of *Catholicism.*

Father McBrien discusses the new Rite of Reconciliation at p. 841 of *Catholicism,* and the new rite of the Anointing of the Sick at p. 847.

Letter 15: Last Things

Elizabeth Johnson covers the Assumption in her article Assumption of the Blessed Virgin Mary in *Encyc/Harper,* p.104.

The quotation from Richard McBrien on the Beatific Vision is at p.1166 of *Catholicism.*

The theologian Karl Rahner describes death as an act, a self-realization which embodies what a person has made of himself or herself during life. The philosopher Martin Heidegger saw death as bringing responsibility and seriousness to life, and a sense of coherence and purpose. We do not have unlimited time at our disposal, and death exposes the superficiality and triviality of much of what we count as important.

Rahner argues that time came into the world from eternity because it is essential that human beings have the freedom to say yes or no to life and love and the grace of God, and to become mature and responsible, but that the exercise of this freedom must have a final validity which comes to the person *through death.* Eternity is not the continuation of time. It is the stoppage of time in the final validation of all creation. History does not continue into infinity. Life in God is living in the timeless present moment.

The reference to Heidegger is found at p. 1161 of *Catholicism.* For Rahner on death, see his article in *Sacramentum Mundi,* pp. 329-333, and his discussion in *Foundations of Christian Faith, pp. 269-274.*

The reference to Monika Hellwig is from p. 364 of her article on Eschatology in *Systematic Theology, Vol. II.*

The quotation on purgatory is on p. 1070 of Joseph Dinoia's article on purgatory in *Encyc/Harper.*

Schillebeeckx's theory on the death of an evil person is discussed by Thomas Rausch in his *Catholicism* at p. 194.

On the possibly symbolic nature of Satan, see J. Ford's article on Satan in *Encyc/Harper,* p.1163.

For a discussion of angels generally, see Joseph Blenkinsopp's article on Angels in *Encyc/Harper,* p.46.

The general resurrection is discussed in John R. Sach's article in *Encyc/Harper* at pp. 1110-1111.

Richard McBrien discusses the last judgment at pp. 1163-1164 of *Catholicism,* and integrates the final realization of the Kingdom of God and of the Communion of Saints at p.1179.

The final reference to Monika Hellwig is from p.363 of her article on Eschatology in *Systematic Theology,Vol.II.*

Letter 16: Self, Virtue, and Morality

The discussion of "self" in this letter is based on a personal interview with Donald L. Harr, M.D., a practicing psychiatrist and a practicing Christian. See also McBrien, *Christianity,* p. 928 quoting the psychologist Erik Erikson to the effect that ego strength is the equivalent of virtue in that it maintains a balance between the *id* and the *superego.*

The definitions of prudence, justice and temperance are taken from Brid Long's article on Virtue in *Encyc/Liturgical,* pp. 901-902. The definition of courage is from McBrien, *Catholicism,* p. 951.

The definition of faith is based upon Monika Hellwig's article on Faith, *Encyc/Liturgical,* pp. 309-310. The definition of hope is based upon McBrien, *Catholicism,* p.1241. The definition of love is my own.

The definitions of the "three other virtues" are my own, except that peace is defined in Juliana M. Casey's article on Peace in *Encyc/Liturgical*, and in McBrien at pp.926 et. seq.

Most of the material on morality is taken from McBrien's chapter on Foundations of Christian Morality, *Catholicism*, pp. 921-980. The quotation, "To obey [one's conscience] is the very dignity of the human person; according to it the person will be judged etc." is taken from the Vatican II document, *The Church in the Modern World*, n. 16.

Letter 17: Catholic Spirituality

On spirituality generally, see Michael Downey's article Christian Spirituality in *Encyc/Liturgical*, and Thomas Rausch's *Catholicism*, pp. 171-172.

The quote from Anne LaMott is from *Traveling Mercies* (New York: Anchor Books, 1999).

Centering prayer and contemplative prayer generally are thoroughly developed in Thomas Keating's *Open Mind, Open Heart* (Warwick,N.Y. :Amity House, 1986).

The reference to Henry Nouwen is from his book, *Life of the Beloved* (New York: Crossroads, 1992).

See McBrien, *Catholicism*, for the definitions of habitual and actual grace.

I have adapted the ideas on the grace of the present moment from the writings of Abbot Keating and Father Richard J. Hopkins.

The statements and quotation from Roger Haight are from his article on Sin and Grace found in Volume II, *Systematic Theology*

The quotation from Congar is found at p, vii of Vol. I of *I Believe in the Holy Spirit* (New York: The Seabury Press, 1983).

The Ellsberg book is found at New York: North Point Press, 2003.

The reference to happiness is from McBrien.

Letter 18: Catholic Lifestyle

The quote from Abbot Keating is from his monograph in *Contemplative Outreach News,* Volume 10, Number 11, Spring 1996 (Butler, New Jersey: Contemplative Outreach, Ltd.).

Joseph G. Allegretti frequently uses the term "the spirituality of the ordinary" in his book on work and the spiritual life, *Loving Your Job, Finding Your Passion* (New York: Paulist Press, 2000). His quotation is at p. 128.

See also, Michael Novak, *Business as a Calling* (New York: Free Press, 1996).

The quotation from Teilhard de Chardin is from *The Divine Mileu* (New York: Harper & Row, 1957).

Christian Family Life, by Elizabeth McNamer (Billings, Montana: Rimrock Publishing Company, 1976) contains a wealth of ideas for celebrating the seasons and the holidays with young children.